How to Heal What You Can't Forget

A Roadmap to Releasing the Past, Embracing Pain, and Building a Life of Peace Again

LAURA DAVISON

As a therapist specializing in trauma recovery, I've read countless books on the subject, but "How to Heal What You Can't Forget" stands in a league of its own. This book isn't just a collection of theories; it's a lifeline, a roadmap, a toolkit for anyone grappling with the lingering effects of past wounds. The author's compassionate voice and practical guidance have empowered me to not only heal my own traumas but also to better support my clients on their journeys to wholeness. ~ **Dr. James Anderson**, *Therapist*

I picked up this book with a heavy heart, carrying the weight of childhood trauma that had haunted me for decades. I was skeptical, having tried countless therapies and self-help books with little success. But "How to Heal What You Can't Forget" offered a fresh perspective, a new way of understanding my pain and a path towards healing that felt both gentle and empowering. Through the simple yet profound practices outlined in this book,

I have begun to release the grip of the past, to embrace my pain as a teacher, and to cultivate a newfound sense of self-compassion. This book is a gift, a beacon of hope for anyone who has ever felt trapped by the past. ~ **Joanna Johnson**, *Teacher*

I've always struggled with anxiety and a sense of disconnection from my body. After reading "How to Heal What You Can't Forget," I began to understand the link between my emotional and physical well-being. The somatic practices outlined in this book have been transformative, helping me to release tension, connect with my body's wisdom, and find a sense of grounding and peace that I never thought possible. This book is a treasure trove of practical tools and insights that have truly changed my life. ~ **Smith Davis**, *Engineer*

As a survivor of domestic violence, I felt like my story was defined by pain and fear. But "How to

Heal What You Can't Forget" helped me to rewrite my narrative, to see myself not as a victim, but as a survivor. The author's compassionate guidance and practical exercises empowered me to reclaim my power, to embrace my pain as a teacher, and to create a new chapter in my life filled with hope, healing, and joy. This book is a must-read for anyone who wants to break free from the chains of the past and create a brighter future. ~ **Jessica Brown**, *Artist*

Dedication

To the courageous souls who carry the weight of what they cannot forget, who dare to face their pain and seek the light of healing. This book is dedicated to you, your resilience, and your unwavering spirit. May these pages serve as a companion on your journey, a source of solace, and a testament to the transformative power that lies within your wounds. May you find the strength to rewrite your story, to embrace your pain as a teacher, and to create a life of peace, joy, and unwavering hope.

Acknowledgements

With heartfelt gratitude, I acknowledge the countless individuals who have bravely shared their stories of trauma and healing, illuminating the path for others. Your courage, resilience, and unwavering spirit have been a constant source of inspiration throughout the writing of this book.

I extend my deepest appreciation to the therapists, healers, and researchers who have dedicated their lives to understanding the complexities of trauma and developing innovative approaches to healing. Your wisdom and expertise have been invaluable in shaping the content of this book.

To my family and friends, thank you for your unwavering love, support, and encouragement. Your belief in me has been a constant source of strength throughout this journey.

To my editor, agent, and publisher, thank you for your guidance, expertise, and unwavering belief in this project. Your collaboration has been instrumental in bringing this book to life.

Finally, to the readers who have picked up this book, I hope that these pages offer you solace, guidance, and inspiration on your own healing journey. May you find the courage to face your pain, the wisdom to learn from your experiences, and the strength to create a life of peace, joy, and unwavering hope.

CopyRight ©

All rights reserved. No part of this book may be reproduced, stored in a retrieval system, or transmitted in any form or by any means, electronic, mechanical, photocopying, recording, scanning, or otherwise, without the written permission of the publisher. Except for brief quotations in a review, scholarly work, or use in connection with a permitted transformative work embodying originality sufficient to merit independent protection, copyright protection subsists in all forms, media, and technologies of expression now known or later developed.

LAURA DAVISON © 2024

Why This Book?

Are you haunted by memories you can't erase? Do you find yourself reliving past traumas, their sting as sharp as the day they occurred? Does the weight of the past hold you back from experiencing joy, peace, and fulfillment in the present?

If so, this book is for you.

"How to Heal What You Can't Forget" is a compassionate and empowering guide for anyone who has ever felt trapped by the past. It's a roadmap to releasing the pain, rewriting your story, and building a life of peace and resilience.

This book is not about forgetting. It's about healing. It's about acknowledging the wounds you carry, honoring your experiences, and finding ways to integrate them into your life in a way that empowers you, rather than diminishes you.

Within these pages, you will discover:

The science of trauma: How trauma affects the mind, body, and spirit, and why some memories refuse to fade.

The power of acknowledgment: Why facing your pain is essential for healing, and how to do it in a safe and supportive way.

The gift of forgiveness: How to release resentment and anger, both towards yourself and others, and open your heart to healing.

The wisdom in your wounds: How to reframe your experiences, identify valuable lessons, and transform your pain into purpose.

The healing power of mindfulness and self-compassion: How to cultivate a kind and loving relationship with yourself, and find peace in the present moment.

The art of building resilience: How to develop the inner strength and coping mechanisms to navigate life's challenges and setbacks.

The importance of connection: How to build a supportive network of relationships and find your tribe of fellow healers.

The power of rewriting your story: How to reclaim your identity, envision a brighter future, and create a life that aligns with your values and aspirations.

This book is not a quick fix or a magic bullet. Healing is a journey, not a destination. But with the tools, insights, and strategies offered in these pages, you can embark on a transformative path towards a life of peace, joy, and unwavering hope.

If you're ready to let go of the past, to embrace your pain as a teacher, and to create a new chapter in your life, then this book is for you. It's time to reclaim your power, rewrite your story, and heal what you can't forget.

How To Use This Book

This book is not a magic wand, nor is it a one-size-fits-all prescription. It's a compass, a map, a toolbox designed to guide you on your unique journey to healing what you can't forget. It's an invitation to embark on a transformative adventure, to delve into the depths of your pain, and to emerge stronger, wiser, and more whole.

Approach this book with an open heart and a curious mind. Allow yourself to be vulnerable, to explore the uncomfortable corners of your past, and to embrace the full spectrum of your emotions. Remember, healing is not a linear process. There will be days when you feel empowered and days when you feel discouraged. Be patient with yourself, honor your pace, and trust that you are exactly where you need to be on your journey.

Don't feel obligated to read this book cover to cover. Instead, use it as a resource, a guide to consult as needed. Dip into the chapters that resonate most deeply with you, revisit sections that offer particular insights, and skip over anything that doesn't feel relevant at this time. For those who will want to begin this journey with chapter that resonate most with them, some aforementioned information may be repeated so that you will have complete understanding. This book is yours to explore, to personalize, to make your own.

Consider keeping a journal alongside your reading. Use it to reflect on the questions posed, to record your insights and realizations, and to track your progress. Journaling can be a powerful tool for processing emotions, making sense of your experiences, and creating a new narrative for your life.

Engage with the exercises and practices offered in this book. Experiment with different techniques, find what works for you, and incorporate them into your daily routine. Remember, healing is an active process. It requires effort, commitment, and a willingness to step outside of your comfort zone.

Reach out for support when you need it. Whether it's a trusted friend, family member, therapist, or support group, connecting with others who understand your experiences can be a lifeline on your healing journey. Remember, you are not alone.

Most importantly, be kind to yourself. Healing is a process, not a destination. There will be setbacks, challenges, and moments of doubt. But with each step you take, with each act of self-compassion, you are moving closer to a life of peace, joy, and liberation. Embrace your healing journey, and trust that it will lead you to a brighter tomorrow.

Contents

Dedication i

Acknowledgements vi

CopyRight © viii

Why This Book? ix

How To Use This Book xii

Contents xv

INTRODUCTION 1

The Paradox of Unforgettable Pain 1

The Promise of Healing: A Roadmap to Peace 5

Chapter 1: Understanding the Wounds We Carry 11

The Many Faces of Trauma: Big T and Little t... 16

How Trauma Impacts the Mind, Body, and Spirit 20

Chapter 2: Releasing the Grip of the Past . 26

The Power of Acknowledgment: Facing Your Pain 31

Forgiveness: A Gift to Yourself, Not Just Others 35

Self-Reflection Questions: 40

Transformative Exercises: 41

Chapter 3: Embracing Your Pain as a Teacher 43

The Wisdom in Your Wounds: Lessons Learned 48

Transforming Pain into Purpose and Growth....53

Self-Reflection Questions: 57

Transformative Exercises: 57

Chapter 4: The Healing Power of Mindfulness 60

Being Present: Anchoring Yourself in the Now .65

Mindful Practices for Trauma Recovery 69

Self-Reflection Questions: 74

Transformative Exercises: 74

Chapter 5: Cultivating Self-Compassion 77

The Antidote to Self-Blame: Befriending Yourself
.... 82

Practices for Self-Care and Nurturing 85

Self-Reflection Questions: 90

Transformative Exercises: 91

Chapter 6: Building Resilience: The Art of Bouncing Back 94

Developing Inner Strength: Tools for Coping ... 98

Post-Traumatic Growth: Finding Meaning in Adversity 102

Self-Reflection Questions: 107

Transformative Exercises: 108

Chapter 7: Reconnecting with Your Body . 111

The Mind-Body Connection: Healing from the Inside Out 115

Somatic Practices for Trauma Release 120

Self-Reflection Questions: 125

Transformative Exercises: 126

Chapter 8: Healing Through Connection . 129

The Importance of Safe Relationships: Building a Support Network 133

Finding Your Tribe: Community and Healing . 138

Self-Reflection Questions: 142

Transformative Exercises: 143

Chapter 9: Rewriting Your Story 146

Reframing Your Narrative: From Victim to Survivor 151

Creating a New Chapter: Envisioning Your Future 155

Self-Reflection Questions: 159

Transformative Exercises: 160

Chapter 10: Finding Peace in the Present Moment 162

Gratitude: The Key to Contentment 166

The Art of Letting Go: Surrendering to What Is 170

Self-Reflection Questions: 174

Transformative Exercises: 175

Chapter 11: Building a Life of Peace and Purpose 178

Living in Alignment with Your Values 183

Service to Others: Healing Through Helping ... 187

Chapter 12: The Ongoing Journey: Maintaining Your Peace 192

Relapse Prevention: Navigating Triggers and Challenges 196

The Gift of Healing: Sharing Your Wisdom 200

Conclusion: Embrace Your Healing Journey .. 204

INTRODUCTION

The Paradox of Unforgettable Pain

"The wound is the place where the Light enters you." - Rumi

There exists a curious paradox within the human spirit: the tenacious grip of memory on events we desperately wish to erase. We are creatures of recollection, our minds etched with the imprints of our past. Yet, some memories refuse to fade, lingering like shadows in the corners of our consciousness. These are the memories of pain, of trauma, of loss – the ones that sting with a sharpness that time seems unable to dull. We yearn to forget, to move on, to rewrite the narrative of our lives. But these memories, these wounds, refuse to be ignored. They cling to us, shaping our thoughts, emotions, and even our physical health.

The weight of unhealed pain can be a heavy burden to bear. It manifests in a myriad of ways, leaving its mark on our emotional landscape. We may find ourselves grappling with anxiety, depression, or anger, our inner world a storm of turmoil. Our relationships may suffer, as we build walls to protect ourselves from further hurt. We may struggle to find joy in the present, haunted by the ghosts of the past. The psychological toll is immense, leaving us feeling trapped in a cycle of suffering.

But the impact of unresolved trauma extends beyond the realm of emotions. It seeps into our very bodies, leaving a trail of physical ailments in its wake. Chronic pain, fatigue, digestive issues, and a weakened immune system can all be linked to the stress of unhealed wounds. Our bodies, once vibrant and resilient, become battlegrounds for the war raging within. We may find ourselves caught in a vicious cycle, where emotional pain triggers physical symptoms, which in turn exacerbate the emotional distress.

Sarah, a vibrant young woman with a contagious laugh, carried a secret burden. Behind her cheerful facade lay a childhood marred by neglect and emotional abuse. Though she had achieved success in her career and built a loving family, the echoes of her past haunted her. She struggled with chronic anxiety and insomnia, her body bearing the scars of her unhealed wounds. Sarah longed to break free from the chains of her past, to reclaim her life and find peace. But the memories, like stubborn weeds, refused to be uprooted.

Similarly, John, a war veteran, carried the weight of his experiences on the battlefield. The horrors he had witnessed had left an indelible mark on his soul. Nightmares plagued his sleep, and flashbacks transported him back to the trenches. He isolated himself from loved ones, convinced that they could never understand the depths of his pain. John yearned to shed the armor he had built around his heart and find solace in the company of others. But the memories, like shrapnel embedded in his flesh, continued to cause him pain.

These stories are not unique. They are echoes of countless others who bear the burden of unhealed wounds. The longing for healing is a universal human experience, a testament to our innate resilience and capacity for growth. But the path to healing is not always clear. It is a winding road, filled with twists and turns, setbacks and triumphs. It requires courage, perseverance, and a willingness to confront the pain that we so desperately wish to forget.

The paradox of unforgettable pain is that it can be both a source of immense suffering and a catalyst for profound transformation. Our wounds, though painful, can become wellsprings of wisdom, resilience, and compassion. They can teach us about our strength, our vulnerability, and our capacity for love. They can inspire us to reach out to others, to offer support and understanding to those who are also struggling. In the words of the poet Rumi, "The wound is the place where the Light enters you." It is through our wounds that we can find our greatest strength, our deepest connection to others, and our most profound sense of purpose.

The journey to healing what we can't forget is a deeply personal one. There is no one-size-fits-all approach. But there is hope. There is healing. There is a way to transform our pain into power, to turn our wounds into wisdom, and to build a life of peace and resilience.

The Promise of Healing: A Roadmap to Peace

"Though no one can go back and make a brand new start, anyone can start from now and make a brand new ending." – Carl Bard

The human experience is a tapestry of moments, some joyful, some painful. While the joyous ones often linger in our hearts, the painful ones can embed themselves in our minds, refusing to fade with time. It's a universal truth that some things, no matter how much we yearn to, we simply cannot forget.

Yet, within this seeming impasse lies an empowering truth – we can heal. Healing is not about erasing the past but rather about transforming our relationship with it. It's a journey, not a destination, a continuous process of growth and understanding. It's about embracing the reality that our past experiences, both positive and negative, have shaped us into who we are today.

This book, "How to Heal What You Can't Forget," is your companion on this transformative journey. It's a roadmap designed to guide you through the intricate landscape of healing, offering tools, insights, and strategies to help you release the past, embrace your pain, and ultimately build a life of peace.

The road to healing may be winding, with twists and turns, ups and downs. But rest assured, it is a path well-trodden by countless others who have emerged from the darkness of their past into the light of a brighter future. This book will illuminate that path for you, revealing the signposts, the pitfalls, and the oases of respite along the way.

We'll embark on this journey by first understanding the wounds we carry. We'll delve into the nature of trauma, both big and small, and explore how it impacts our minds, bodies, and spirits. We'll uncover the hidden ways in which unhealed pain can manifest in our lives, from emotional turmoil to physical ailments.

Next, we'll explore the power of acknowledgment and forgiveness. We'll learn how facing our pain, rather than suppressing it, can be the first step towards liberation. We'll discover how forgiveness, both of ourselves and others, can release us from the shackles of resentment and anger.

In the heart of this journey, we'll embrace the profound wisdom that lies within our pain. We'll learn to view our wounds not as sources of shame but as opportunities for growth and transformation. We'll uncover the hidden gifts that lie within our struggles, the resilience, the compassion, the deepened understanding of the human experience.

As we move forward, we'll explore the transformative power of mindfulness and self-compassion. We'll learn to anchor ourselves in the present moment, finding solace in the simple act of being. We'll cultivate a gentle, loving relationship with ourselves, replacing self-criticism with kindness and understanding.

The journey will also take us through the realms of resilience and self-care. We'll equip ourselves with tools to cope with triggers and setbacks, fostering inner strength and the ability to bounce back from adversity. We'll learn to prioritize our well-being, nourishing our bodies and minds with practices that promote healing and restoration.

As we near the end of our journey, we'll focus on rewriting our story. We'll challenge the narratives that have held us captive, reclaiming our power and embracing a new, empowering identity. We'll set our sights on a future filled with peace, purpose, and joy, creating a life that reflects our deepest values and aspirations.

Throughout this book, you'll find real-life stories of individuals who have walked a similar path, their experiences offering inspiration and hope. You'll encounter practical exercises and techniques that you can incorporate into your daily life, supporting your journey toward healing.

Remember, healing is not a linear process. It's a dance of progress and setbacks, of breakthroughs and moments of doubt. But with each step you take, with each challenge you overcome, you'll move closer to the life you envision – a life of peace, resilience, and unwavering hope.

"How to Heal What You Can't Forget" is not just a book; it's an invitation to embark on a transformative adventure. It's a call to embrace your pain, your past, and your whole self. It's a promise that even amidst the deepest wounds, healing is possible. The journey may be long, but the reward is immeasurable – a life lived in harmony with your true self, a life of peace, purpose, and enduring joy.

Chapter 1: Understanding the Wounds We Carry

"The greatest weapon against stress is our ability to choose one thought over another." – William James

The journey to healing begins with understanding. Understanding not just the events that have shaped us, but the profound ways in which those events have left their mark on our minds, bodies, and souls. It begins with recognizing the wounds we carry, the invisible scars that shape our thoughts, emotions, and behaviors.

Research shows that a staggering number of individuals have experienced some form of trauma in their lives. The Adverse Childhood Experiences (ACE) Study, a groundbreaking research project, found that nearly two-thirds of participants had experienced at least one adverse childhood event, such as abuse, neglect, or household dysfunction. These experiences, whether they occurred in childhood or later in life, can leave a lasting imprint on our well-being.

But trauma isn't always a singular, catastrophic event. It can also be the result of ongoing stress, neglect, or even subtle emotional injuries that accumulate over time. These "small t" traumas, while often overlooked or minimized, can be just as damaging as the more obvious "big T" traumas. They can chip away at our resilience, erode our self-worth, and leave us feeling disconnected from ourselves and others.

The impact of trauma is not merely psychological; it's deeply embedded in our biology. When we experience a traumatic event, our bodies go into survival mode, releasing a cascade of stress hormones like cortisol and adrenaline. These hormones prepare us to fight, flee, or freeze in the face of danger. However, when the threat is ongoing or unresolved, this stress response can become chronic, leading to a host of physical and mental health problems.

Unresolved trauma can manifest in a variety of ways, from anxiety and depression to chronic pain and autoimmune disorders. It can disrupt our sleep, impair our memory, and make it difficult to concentrate. It can also lead to unhealthy coping mechanisms, such as substance abuse or self-harm, as we try to numb the pain or regain a sense of control.

But perhaps the most insidious effect of trauma is the way it can distort our perception of ourselves and the world around us. We may develop negative core beliefs about ourselves, believing that we are unworthy, unlovable, or fundamentally flawed. We may view the world as a dangerous place, always on guard for potential threats. These distorted beliefs can lead to self-sabotaging behaviors, unhealthy relationships, and a persistent sense of unease and disconnection.

Understanding the wounds we carry is not about dwelling on the past or wallowing in self-pity. It's about acknowledging the reality of our experiences and the ways in which they have shaped us. It's about recognizing the patterns of thought, emotion, and behavior that stem from our unhealed pain. This awareness is the first step towards healing. It allows us to see ourselves with compassion and understanding, to break free from the grip of our past, and to create a new narrative for our lives.

Consider the story of Maria, a successful executive who struggled with crippling self-doubt. Despite her accomplishments, she felt like a fraud, constantly fearing that she would be exposed as incompetent. Through therapy, Maria discovered that her self-doubt stemmed from a childhood marked by criticism and conditional love. By understanding the roots of her insecurity, she was able to challenge her negative beliefs, develop self-compassion, and embrace her worthiness.

Or take the case of David, a war veteran who suffered from debilitating flashbacks and nightmares. He isolated himself from loved ones, convinced that they could never understand the horrors he had witnessed. Through trauma-focused therapy and support groups, David began to heal. He learned to manage his triggers, to process his emotions in healthy ways, and to reconnect with the people who cared about him.

These stories illustrate the power of understanding. When we delve into the depths of our wounds, we can uncover the hidden mechanisms that drive our thoughts and behaviors. We can begin to make sense of our experiences, to integrate them into our life story, and to move forward with greater clarity and purpose.

The Many Faces of Trauma: Big T and Little t

"Trauma creates change you don't choose. Healing is about creating change you do choose." – Michelle Rosenthal

The word "trauma" often conjures images of catastrophic events: natural disasters, violent crimes, or horrific accidents. These are the "Big T" traumas, the experiences that shatter our sense of safety and leave us reeling in their wake. But trauma isn't always so easily defined or identified. It can also manifest in subtler, less obvious ways, through events that may not seem life-threatening but nevertheless leave a lasting impact on our well-being. These are the "little t" traumas, the everyday wounds that can chip away at our resilience and erode our sense of self.

Big T traumas are the events that make headlines and dominate our collective consciousness. They are the earthquakes, the terrorist attacks, the wars that leave entire communities devastated. They are the car accidents, the assaults, the sudden losses that shatter our individual worlds. These events, with their sheer scale and intensity, can overwhelm our coping mechanisms and leave us feeling powerless and vulnerable.

But not all traumas are so dramatic. Little t traumas are the subtle, insidious wounds that can occur in the context of everyday life. They may not be life-threatening, but they can still be deeply distressing and have long-lasting effects. These include experiences like emotional neglect, bullying, verbal abuse, discrimination, or even the repeated witnessing of violence. They can also be the result of ongoing stressors, such as financial hardship, chronic illness, or relationship difficulties.

The distinction between Big T and little t traumas is not always clear-cut. What may be a minor event for one person can be profoundly traumatic for another, depending on their individual experiences, vulnerabilities, and support systems. Moreover, both types of trauma can leave lasting scars and impact our well-being in similar ways.

Both Big T and little t traumas can trigger a stress response in our bodies, releasing a flood of hormones that prepare us to fight, flee, or freeze. This response, while adaptive in the short term, can become problematic when it persists long after the threat has passed. Chronic stress can wreak havoc on our physical health, leading to a range of ailments, including cardiovascular disease, diabetes, and autoimmune disorders.

The psychological impact of trauma is equally profound. Both Big T and little t traumas can disrupt our sense of safety, security, and trust in the world. They can lead to anxiety, depression, post-traumatic stress disorder (PTSD), and other mental health conditions. They can also erode our self-esteem, leaving us feeling worthless, helpless, or fundamentally flawed.

Consider the story of Emily, a successful businesswoman who struggled with chronic anxiety and panic attacks. For years, she couldn't pinpoint the source of her distress. Through therapy, she discovered that her anxiety stemmed from a childhood marked by emotional neglect and constant criticism from her parents. While her experiences didn't fit the classic definition of trauma, they had nevertheless left a deep imprint on her psyche, shaping her beliefs about herself and the world.

Or take the case of Michael, a naval officer who struggled with nightmares, flashbacks, and hypervigilance. He sought help for PTSD, but his therapist also discovered that Michael had been bullied relentlessly throughout his childhood. The constant taunting and humiliation had eroded his sense of self-worth and left him feeling vulnerable and insecure. It became clear that both the war trauma and the childhood bullying had contributed to his current struggles.

These stories illustrate that trauma is not a one-size-fits-all phenomenon. It comes in many forms, shapes, and sizes. It can be a single, overwhelming event or a series of smaller, seemingly insignificant experiences. But regardless of its form, trauma can leave lasting scars on our minds, bodies, and spirits.

Understanding the many faces of trauma is an essential first step on the path to healing. It allows us to see our experiences in a new light, to acknowledge the impact they have had on us, and to begin the process of recovery. It reminds us that we are not alone in our struggles and that healing is possible, even from the deepest wounds.

How Trauma Impacts the Mind, Body, and Spirit

"Trauma is not just an event that took place sometime in the past; it is also the imprint left by that experience on mind, brain, and body." – Bessel van der Kolk

Trauma, whether a single life-altering event or a series of ongoing stressors, leaves an enduring mark on the human experience. Its impact reverberates through our minds, bodies, and spirits, altering the very fabric of our being. Understanding the science behind this impact is crucial to embarking on the path to healing.

When we experience trauma, our brains and bodies go into survival mode. The amygdala, the brain's alarm system, signals a threat, triggering a cascade of stress hormones, including cortisol and adrenaline. These hormones prepare us to fight, flee, or freeze, priming our bodies for immediate action. However, when the threat persists or remains unresolved, this stress response can become chronic, leading to a state of hyperarousal and dysregulation.

In the aftermath of trauma, the brain's hippocampus, responsible for memory consolidation and contextualization, can shrink, making it difficult to distinguish between past and present threats. This can lead to flashbacks, nightmares, and intrusive thoughts, as the brain relives the traumatic event as if it were happening in the present moment. The prefrontal cortex, responsible for rational thought and decision-making, may also become less active, making it harder to regulate emotions and cope with stress.

The nervous system, too, bears the brunt of trauma. The autonomic nervous system, which controls involuntary bodily functions like heart rate and breathing, can become dysregulated, leading to symptoms like hypervigilance, panic attacks, and difficulty sleeping. The immune system can also be compromised, leaving us more susceptible to illness and disease.

The impact of trauma on the body is not merely theoretical; it's measurable and observable. Studies have shown that individuals with a history of trauma are more likely to experience chronic pain, fatigue, digestive problems, and other physical ailments. They may also be at higher risk for developing chronic diseases like heart disease, stroke, and diabetes.

The emotional and psychological consequences of trauma are equally significant. Trauma can shatter our sense of safety, leaving us feeling vulnerable, anxious, and on edge. It can erode our self-esteem, making us feel worthless, helpless, or fundamentally flawed. It can also disrupt our relationships, making it difficult to trust others or form meaningful connections.

Trauma can manifest as a range of emotional and psychological symptoms, including:

- **Anxiety:** A persistent feeling of worry, fear, or unease, often accompanied by physical symptoms like racing heart, sweating, and difficulty breathing.

- **Depression:** A pervasive sense of sadness, hopelessness, and loss of interest in activities that were once enjoyable.

- **Post-Traumatic Stress Disorder (PTSD):** A complex mental health condition characterized by flashbacks, nightmares, hypervigilance, and avoidance of trauma-related stimuli.

- **Anger and irritability:** A heightened sense of anger or frustration, often triggered by seemingly minor events.

- **Guilt and shame:** Feelings of self-blame or worthlessness, often stemming from the belief that one could have prevented or changed the traumatic event.

- **Dissociation:** A feeling of detachment from oneself or one's surroundings, often used as a coping mechanism to numb emotional pain.

Trauma can also lead to unhealthy coping mechanisms, such as substance abuse or self-harm. These behaviors may provide temporary relief from emotional pain, but they ultimately perpetuate the cycle of suffering and hinder the healing process.

The impact of trauma on the spirit is perhaps the most difficult to quantify, yet it is no less real or significant. Trauma can shatter our sense of meaning and purpose, leaving us feeling lost, disconnected, and adrift. It can erode our faith in the goodness of humanity and our belief in a just and loving universe. It can also lead to a sense of isolation and alienation, as we feel that no one can truly understand what we've been through.

However, it's important to remember that trauma does not have to define us. While its impact is undeniable, it does not have the final say. The human spirit is remarkably resilient, capable of healing and growth even in the face of immense adversity. By understanding the ways in which trauma affects us, we can begin to unravel its grip and reclaim our lives. We can learn to manage our symptoms, develop healthy coping mechanisms, and cultivate a renewed sense of meaning and purpose. We can emerge from the darkness of trauma stronger, wiser, and more compassionate than before.

Chapter 2: Releasing the Grip of the Past

"The past is a place of reference, not a place of residence." – Roy T. Bennett

The weight of the past can be a heavy anchor, tethering us to pain, regret, and resentment. It can feel like a relentless undertow, pulling us back into the depths of our wounds. But healing is not about erasing the past; it's about transforming our relationship with it. It's about acknowledging its impact, learning from its lessons, and ultimately, releasing its grip on our present and future.

The journey to releasing the past begins with a radical act of honesty – the willingness to face our pain. For many of us, this is a daunting prospect. We've spent years building walls around our hearts, burying our emotions deep beneath layers of denial and avoidance. We fear that if we allow ourselves to feel the full weight of our pain, we will be overwhelmed, consumed by it. But the truth is, the only way out is through. By facing our pain head-on, we create space for healing to occur.

This doesn't mean wallowing in self-pity or dwelling on the past. It means acknowledging the reality of our experiences, validating our emotions, and giving ourselves permission to grieve, to rage, to feel whatever needs to be felt. It means allowing the tears to flow, the anger to rise, the sadness to wash over us. By allowing ourselves to fully experience our emotions, we can begin to integrate them into our lives, rather than letting them fester in the shadows.

One powerful tool for releasing the past is forgiveness. Forgiveness is not about condoning the actions of those who have hurt us, nor is it about forgetting or minimizing the pain they have caused. It's about choosing to let go of the anger, resentment, and bitterness that keep us tethered to the past. It's about freeing ourselves from the cycle of blame and victimhood.

Forgiveness is a gift we give ourselves, not just others. When we hold onto anger and resentment, we are the ones who suffer the most. We carry the burden of those emotions with us, poisoning our relationships, our health, and our overall well-being. By choosing to forgive, we are not excusing the harm that has been done, but rather freeing ourselves from its toxic grip.

Forgiveness can be a challenging process, especially when the wounds are deep. It takes time, patience, and a willingness to confront our own vulnerabilities. It may involve setting boundaries, seeking support from loved ones or professionals, and engaging in practices like journaling, meditation, or therapy. But the rewards are immeasurable. When we forgive, we open ourselves up to the possibility of healing, growth, and inner peace.

Consider the story of Anna, a woman who had been deeply wounded by her husband's infidelity. For years, she held onto her anger and resentment, replaying the events in her mind over and over again. She felt betrayed, humiliated, and consumed by a thirst for revenge. But as time went on, she realized that her anger was only hurting her. It was preventing her from moving on, from rebuilding her life, and from finding happiness again.

With the help of a therapist, Anna began the process of forgiveness. It wasn't easy, but gradually, she was able to let go of her anger and resentment. She came to understand that her husband's actions were a reflection of his own struggles and insecurities, not a reflection of her worth. By forgiving him, she was able to forgive herself for not seeing the warning signs and for staying in a relationship that was no longer serving her.

Anna's story is a testament to the transformative power of forgiveness. It's not about condoning or excusing the harm that has been done, but rather about choosing to release the negative emotions that keep us trapped in the past. By forgiving, we are not only freeing ourselves from the burden of anger and resentment, but we are also opening ourselves up to the possibility of healing, growth, and a renewed sense of inner peace. We'll discuss more on forgiveness later in this chapter.

Releasing the grip of the past is not a one-time event; it's an ongoing process. There will be days when the memories resurface, when the pain feels as raw as ever. But with each act of acknowledgment, with each step towards forgiveness, we chip away at the walls that have held us captive. We reclaim our power, our agency, and our ability to shape our own future. We move closer to a life where the past is a place of reference, not a place of residence.

The Power of Acknowledgment: Facing Your Pain

"What we cannot hold, we cannot heal." – Ntozake Shange

In the labyrinthine journey of healing, the path often begins with a seemingly paradoxical step: facing the very pain we wish to escape. It's a counterintuitive notion, one that challenges our natural instinct to avoid discomfort. Yet, the profound truth is that what we resist persists. It's only by acknowledging and validating our past pain that we can truly begin to heal.

Denying or suppressing our pain may offer temporary respite, but it ultimately hinders our journey towards wholeness. Unacknowledged pain festers beneath the surface, casting a shadow over our lives. It can manifest in myriad ways, from physical ailments to emotional turmoil, from strained relationships to a pervasive sense of unease. It's like a wound left untreated, slowly festering and infecting the surrounding tissue.

Acknowledging our pain, on the other hand, is akin to cleaning a wound. It's the first step towards recovery, the necessary precursor to healing. When we shine a light on our pain, we bring it out of the shadows and into the realm of consciousness. We give it a voice, a name, a place in our story. This act of acknowledgment validates our experiences, affirming that our pain is real, valid, and worthy of our attention.

Validation is a powerful antidote to shame and self-blame. When we deny our pain, we implicitly tell ourselves that our feelings are wrong, invalid, or unimportant. This can lead to a downward spiral of self-doubt and self-recrimination. But when we validate our pain, we affirm our worthiness of love, compassion, and healing. We give ourselves permission to be human, to feel the full spectrum of emotions, and to seek the support we need.

Identifying and expressing our emotions in healthy ways is a crucial aspect of acknowledging our pain. Many of us have been conditioned to suppress our emotions, to put on a brave face and pretend that everything is okay. But emotions are not meant to be bottled up; they are meant to be felt, processed, and released. When we deny our emotions, they don't simply disappear; they find other ways to express themselves, often in unhealthy and destructive ways.

One way to identify our emotions is to tune into our bodies. Emotions are not just mental states; they are also physical sensations. Anger may manifest as tightness in the chest, fear as a knot in the stomach, sadness as a heaviness in the limbs. By paying attention to our bodily sensations, we can gain valuable insights into our emotional landscape.

Once we have identified our emotions, it's important to find healthy ways to express them. This might involve talking to a trusted friend or therapist, journaling, engaging in creative activities, or simply allowing ourselves to cry or scream. The key is to find outlets that allow us to release the emotional energy without harming ourselves or others.

Another helpful tool for acknowledging and expressing our pain is mindfulness. Mindfulness is the practice of paying attention to the present moment without judgment. It involves observing our thoughts, emotions, and bodily sensations with curiosity and openness. By cultivating mindfulness, we can learn to sit with our pain, to witness it without getting overwhelmed by it. We can begin to see our emotions as passing waves, rather than defining characteristics.

It's important to remember that acknowledging our pain is not a one-time event; it's a continuous engagement. There will be days when the pain feels overwhelming, when the old wounds threaten to reopen. But with practice, we can learn to hold our pain with compassion, to acknowledge it without letting it consume us. We can learn to turn towards our pain, rather than away from it, and in doing so, we can discover a wellspring of strength, resilience, and healing within ourselves.

Forgiveness: A Gift to Yourself, Not Just Others

"To forgive is to set a prisoner free and discover that the prisoner was you." – Lewis B. Smedes

Forgiveness, a concept often shrouded in misconceptions, is a powerful catalyst for healing. It's not about condoning harmful actions or pretending that the pain inflicted upon us didn't happen. Rather, it's a conscious choice to release ourselves from the shackles of resentment, anger, and bitterness that bind us to the past. It's a profound act of self-liberation, a gift we give ourselves on the path to healing and wholeness.

When we harbor resentment and anger towards those who have hurt us, we unwittingly become prisoners of our own pain. We replay the events in our minds, reliving the hurt and fueling our anger. We allow the past to dictate our present and cloud our future. This toxic cycle of rumination and resentment consumes our energy, erodes our peace, and hinders our ability to move forward.

Forgiveness, on the other hand, is a key that unlocks the door to freedom. It allows us to step out of the prison of our pain and into the light of healing. It doesn't mean forgetting or minimizing the wrong that was done, but it does mean choosing to release the negative emotions that keep us tethered to the past. It's about acknowledging that while the actions of others may have caused us pain, we do not have to allow that pain to define us.

The process of forgiveness is not a simple one. It's a journey that requires courage, patience, and a willingness to confront our own vulnerabilities. It begins with understanding – understanding that the person who hurt us is also flawed and human, capable of making mistakes. It involves cultivating empathy, trying to see the situation from their perspective, even if we don't condone their actions. It also requires a willingness to let go, to release the need for revenge or retribution, and to trust that justice will ultimately prevail.

One helpful framework for understanding the process of forgiveness is the REACH model, developed by psychologist Everett Worthington. REACH stands for:

- **Recall:** Recall the hurt objectively, without embellishment or exaggeration.

- **Empathize:** Try to understand the offender's perspective, even if you don't agree with it.

- **Altruistic gift:** Recognize that forgiveness is a gift you give yourself, not the offender.

- **Commit:** Make a conscious decision to forgive, even if you don't feel like it yet.

- **Hold onto forgiveness:** Remember your decision to forgive, even when the pain resurfaces.

This model provides a structured approach to forgiveness, guiding us through the emotional and psychological steps involved. It emphasizes the importance of understanding, empathy, and commitment in the process of letting go.

Forgiveness is not a sign of weakness or a denial of justice. It's a powerful act of self-love and liberation. It allows us to reclaim our power, to break free from the cycle of pain and resentment, and to create space for healing and growth. It's a gift we give ourselves, a pathway to a more peaceful and fulfilling life.

Consider the story of James, a man who was deeply hurt by his father's abandonment. For years, he carried the weight of anger and resentment, blaming his father for his struggles and insecurities. He felt that his father owed him an apology, a recognition of the pain he had caused. But his father was no longer alive, and James realized that holding onto his anger was only hurting him.

Through therapy and self-reflection, James began to understand his father's own struggles and shortcomings. He realized that his father's actions were a reflection of his own unhealed wounds, not a reflection of James' worth. He began to cultivate empathy for his father, seeing him as a flawed human being, rather than a villain.

With time and effort, James was able to forgive his father. He didn't forget the pain, but he chose to release the anger and resentment that had held him captive for so long. This act of forgiveness didn't erase the past, but it transformed James' relationship with it. It allowed him to move forward with a lighter heart, to focus on his own healing and growth, and to build a life free from the shackles of resentment.

James' story illustrates the transformative power of forgiveness. It's not about condoning or excusing the harm that has been done, but rather about choosing to release the negative emotions that keep us trapped in the past. By forgiving, we are not only freeing ourselves from the burden of anger and resentment, but we are also opening ourselves up to the possibility of healing, growth, and a renewed sense of inner peace.

Self-Reflection Questions:

1. What past experiences or traumas am I still holding onto? What emotions are attached to these memories?

2. How do these past experiences affect my thoughts, feelings, and behaviors in the present?

3. What would it feel like to release the anger, resentment, or bitterness associated with these experiences?

4. What steps can I take to acknowledge and validate my pain in a healthy way?

5. Am I willing to explore the concept of forgiveness, both for myself and others? What would that look like for me?

Transformative Exercises:

1. **Journaling:** Write a letter to your past self, acknowledging their pain and offering words of comfort and encouragement.

2. **Meditation:** Practice mindfulness meditation to become more aware of your thoughts and emotions related to past experiences. Observe them without judgment, allowing them to come and go.

3. **Creative Expression:** Express your emotions through art, music, dance, or any other creative outlet that resonates with you.

4. **Forgiveness Letter:** Write a letter to the person who hurt you (you don't have to send it). Express your pain, anger, and hurt, but also offer words of forgiveness. This can be a powerful way to release negative emotions.

5. **Compassion Practice:** Practice self-compassion by speaking to yourself as you would a dear friend who is struggling. Offer

yourself words of kindness, understanding, and support.

Chapter 3: Embracing Your Pain as a Teacher

"Pain is inevitable. Suffering is optional." – Haruki Murakami

In the heart of adversity lies a profound paradox – the potential for growth, wisdom, and transformation. Pain, often perceived as an adversary, can become an unlikely ally on the journey to healing. It is in the crucible of our suffering that we often discover our greatest strengths, our deepest resilience, and our most profound capacity for compassion. Embracing our pain as a teacher is not about glorifying suffering or denying its harsh realities. It's about recognizing the inherent wisdom within our wounds and using it as a catalyst for personal growth.

Throughout history, countless individuals have emerged from the depths of despair transformed by their experiences. Viktor Frankl, a psychiatrist who survived the horrors of the Holocaust, discovered meaning and purpose in the midst of unimaginable suffering. He wrote, "Everything can be taken from a man but one thing: the last of the human freedoms – to choose one's attitude in any given set of circumstances, to choose one's own way." Frankl's experiences taught him that even in the darkest of times, we have the power to find meaning and create a life worth living.

Malala Yousafzai, a young Pakistani activist who was shot in the head by the Taliban for advocating for girls' education, emerged from her ordeal with a renewed sense of purpose and a determination to fight for the rights of others. Her pain became a source of inspiration, fueling her activism and transforming her into a global symbol of courage and resilience.

These stories, and countless others like them, demonstrate that pain is not the end of the story. It can be a turning point, a catalyst for profound personal growth and transformation. When we embrace our pain as a teacher, we open ourselves up to the possibility of post-traumatic growth, a phenomenon in which individuals who have experienced trauma not only recover but actually thrive in the aftermath.

Post-traumatic growth is not about denying the pain or minimizing its impact. It's about recognizing that adversity can be a powerful catalyst for positive change. Individuals who experience post-traumatic growth often report increased resilience, a greater appreciation for life, stronger relationships, a heightened sense of personal strength, and a deeper sense of meaning and purpose.

Embracing pain as a teacher involves a shift in perspective. It requires us to view our wounds not as sources of shame or weakness, but as opportunities for learning and growth. It asks us to ask ourselves, "What can I learn from this experience? How can I use this pain to become a better version of myself?"

This shift in perspective is not easy. It takes courage, vulnerability, and a willingness to confront our deepest fears. It may involve seeking professional help, joining a support group, or engaging in practices like journaling or meditation. But the rewards are immeasurable. When we embrace our pain as a teacher, we open ourselves up to a world of possibility, a world where our wounds can become wellsprings of wisdom, resilience, and compassion.

Consider the story of Sarah, a woman who was diagnosed with a life-threatening illness. Initially, she was consumed by fear, anger, and despair. But as she began to process her emotions and come to terms with her diagnosis, she discovered a newfound appreciation for life. She started volunteering at a local hospice, offering support and comfort to others facing similar challenges. Her pain, while still present, became a source of connection and compassion, allowing her to find meaning and purpose in the midst of adversity.

Or take the case of John, a man who lost his wife in a tragic accident. He was devastated by grief, consumed by guilt and anger. But through therapy and support groups, he learned to channel his pain into creative expression. He began writing poetry, painting, and composing music, using his art as a way to process his emotions and connect with others who had experienced loss. His pain became a source of inspiration, fueling his creativity and helping him to find solace and healing.

These stories illustrate the transformative power of embracing pain as a teacher. They show us that even in the darkest of times, there is potential for growth, healing, and a renewed sense of purpose. By facing our pain head-on, by allowing ourselves to feel the full spectrum of emotions, and by seeking out support when needed, we can transform our wounds into wellsprings of wisdom, resilience, and compassion. We can emerge from the crucible of suffering stronger, wiser, and more connected to ourselves and others.

The Wisdom in Your Wounds: Lessons Learned

"Turn your wounds into wisdom." – Oprah Winfrey

The depths of our pain often hold the seeds of our greatest wisdom. Adversity, while undeniably difficult, can serve as a crucible for growth, forging resilience, compassion, and a deeper understanding of ourselves and the world around us. Within the heart of our wounds lie valuable lessons, waiting to be unearthed and integrated into our lives.

Consider the Japanese art of Kintsugi, where broken pottery is repaired with gold lacquer, highlighting the cracks rather than hiding them. The repaired piece is not only restored to functionality but is also considered more beautiful for having been broken. Similarly, our wounds, though painful, can become sources of strength and beauty, adding depth and richness to our lives.

The wisdom gained from pain is often hard-won, emerging from the crucible of suffering. It's the understanding that comes from facing our deepest fears, overcoming adversity, and persevering through challenges. It's the empathy that arises from experiencing heartbreak, loss, or betrayal. It's the resilience that develops when we pick ourselves up after being knocked down.

Pain can teach us about our own strength and resilience. It can show us that we are capable of enduring more than we ever thought possible. It can reveal hidden reserves of courage and determination that we never knew we possessed. When we face our pain head-on, we discover that we are not victims, but survivors.

Pain can also teach us about our vulnerabilities. It can show us where we need to heal, where we need to grow, and where we need to set boundaries. It can teach us to be more compassionate towards ourselves and others, to recognize the shared human experience of suffering.

Pain can also deepen our understanding of the world around us. It can open our eyes to the injustices and inequalities that exist, inspiring us to work towards a more just and equitable society. It can also lead us to a greater appreciation for the simple joys of life, the beauty of nature, the love of family and friends.

Reframing our experiences is a powerful tool for extracting wisdom from our wounds. Instead of viewing our pain as a curse, we can choose to see it as a catalyst for growth. We can ask ourselves, "What can I learn from this experience? How can I use this pain to become a better version of myself?"

For example, if we've experienced betrayal, we might learn the importance of setting healthy boundaries and choosing our relationships wisely. If we've faced a health challenge, we might develop a deeper appreciation for our bodies and a commitment to self-care. If we've experienced loss, we might learn to cherish the present moment and to express our love and gratitude more freely.

Identifying the valuable lessons learned from our pain can be a transformative process. It allows us to shift our focus from victimhood to empowerment, from despair to hope. It helps us to see our wounds not as sources of shame or weakness, but as badges of honor, testaments to our resilience and strength.

Consider the story of Natasha, a woman who struggled with chronic pain for years. She felt like her body had betrayed her, and she often fell into despair. But through therapy and mindfulness practices, she learned to listen to her body's signals and to treat herself with compassion. She discovered that her pain was not her enemy, but a messenger, alerting her to areas of her life that needed attention. By embracing her pain as a teacher, Emily was able to transform her relationship with her body and to find a new sense of peace and well-being.

Or take the case of Chris, a man who lost his job and struggled with financial hardship. He felt ashamed and embarrassed, blaming himself for his circumstances. But through support groups and career counseling, he realized that his experience was not unique. He connected with others who had faced similar challenges and learned from their resilience and resourcefulness. David's pain became a catalyst for personal growth, inspiring him to start his own business and to find fulfillment in helping others.

These stories illustrate the power of reframing our experiences and identifying the valuable lessons learned from our pain. They remind us that even in the darkest of times, there is potential for growth, healing, and a renewed sense of purpose. By embracing our pain as a teacher, we can transform our wounds into wellsprings of wisdom, resilience, and compassion. We can emerge from the crucible of suffering stronger, wiser, and more connected to ourselves and others.

Transforming Pain into Purpose and Growth

"Our wounds are often the openings into the best and most beautiful part of us." – David Richo

The alchemists of old sought to transform lead into gold. While their quest may have been rooted in the material world, it speaks to a deeper human aspiration: the desire to transmute pain into something precious, to find meaning and purpose in the face of adversity. This alchemical transformation is not merely a metaphor; it's a lived reality for countless individuals who have turned their wounds into wellsprings of creativity, advocacy, and service to others.

Consider the story of Frida Kahlo, the renowned Mexican painter whose life was marked by physical pain and emotional turmoil. Kahlo suffered from polio as a child and later endured a devastating bus accident that left her with chronic pain and numerous surgeries. Yet, it was through her art that she found solace and expression. Her vibrant self-portraits, often depicting her physical and emotional suffering, became a testament to her resilience and a powerful commentary on the female experience.

Maya Angelou, a celebrated poet, memoirist, and civil rights activist, also transformed her pain into purpose. Angelou's childhood was marked by trauma, including sexual abuse and racial discrimination. Yet, she found her voice through writing, using her words to speak out against injustice and to inspire others to rise above their circumstances. Her poetry and autobiographical works became a beacon of hope for generations, a testament to the power of the human spirit to overcome adversity.

These are just two examples of individuals who have turned their pain into purpose. There are countless others, from everyday heroes who volunteer their time to support others in need to artists, musicians, and writers who use their creative talents to express the depths of human experience.

Channeling pain into creative outlets can be a powerful healing tool. Art, music, writing, and other forms of creative expression provide a safe space to explore and process emotions, to give voice to the unspoken, and to find meaning in the midst of chaos. Through creativity, we can transform our pain into something tangible, something beautiful, something that can connect us to others and inspire hope.

Advocacy, too, can be a transformative path for those who have experienced pain. By speaking out about our experiences, we can raise awareness, challenge stigma, and advocate for change. We can use our voices to empower others, to offer support and solidarity, and to create a world that is more just, compassionate, and inclusive.

Helping others can also be a profound source of healing. When we reach out to those who are struggling, we not only offer them comfort and support, but we also remind ourselves of our own strength and resilience. We discover that our pain can be a source of connection, empathy, and compassion. We learn that we are not alone in our suffering and that by helping others, we can also heal ourselves.

The transformation of pain into purpose is not an overnight process. It requires courage, perseverance, and a willingness to face our wounds head-on. It may involve seeking professional help, joining a support group, or engaging in practices like mindfulness and self-compassion. But the rewards are immeasurable. When we channel our pain into creativity, advocacy, or service to others, we not only heal ourselves, but we also contribute to the healing of the world.

The journey from pain to purpose is a personal one. There is no single path, no one-size-fits-all solution. But the stories of those who have walked this path before us offer inspiration and guidance. They remind us that even in the darkest of times, there is hope, there is healing, and there is the potential for profound transformation.

Self-Reflection Questions:

1. What are the most significant painful experiences I've had in my life? How have these experiences shaped me?

2. What lessons have I learned from these experiences? How have they made me stronger, wiser, or more compassionate?

3. Are there any aspects of my pain that I'm still resisting or denying? What would it look like to embrace these aspects?

4. How can I reframe my past experiences to find meaning and purpose in them?

5. What gifts or strengths have emerged from my struggles? How can I use these gifts to help myself and others?

Transformative Exercises:

1. **Gratitude Journal:** Write down three things you are grateful for each day, even if they seem small or insignificant. This practice

can help shift your focus from pain to appreciation.

2. **Creative Expression:** Engage in a creative activity that allows you to express your emotions, such as writing, painting, drawing, or music. Let your pain flow through your creativity.

3. **Mindfulness Meditation:** Practice mindfulness meditation to cultivate awareness of your thoughts and emotions without judgment. Observe your pain with curiosity and compassion.

4. **Finding Your Voice:** Share your story with a trusted friend, family member, therapist, or support group. Speaking your truth can be a powerful way to heal and connect with others.

5. **Acts of Service:** Volunteer your time, skills, or resources to help others in need. Helping others can shift your focus from your own

pain and provide a sense of purpose and meaning.

Chapter 4: The Healing Power of Mindfulness

"Feelings come and go like clouds in a windy sky. Conscious breathing is my anchor."

In the storm of trauma, the mind can become a whirlwind of thoughts, emotions, and memories. It can feel like being trapped in a relentless cycle of pain, unable to find solace or stillness. But there is a way to anchor ourselves in the present moment, to find a refuge from the turmoil within. That refuge is mindfulness.

Mindfulness, at its core, is the practice of paying attention to the present moment with openness, curiosity, and non-judgment. It's about observing our thoughts, emotions, and bodily sensations without getting caught up in them, allowing them to come and go like waves on the ocean. It's about being fully present in the here and now, not dwelling on the past or worrying about the future.

While mindfulness has its roots in ancient Buddhist traditions, it has gained widespread recognition in recent years for its therapeutic benefits. Numerous studies have shown that mindfulness can reduce stress, anxiety, and depression, improve sleep, boost the immune system, and even enhance overall well-being. For those who have experienced trauma, mindfulness can be a particularly powerful tool for healing.

Trauma often leaves us feeling disconnected from our bodies, our emotions, and the present moment. We may find ourselves ruminating on the past or worrying about the future, our minds racing with anxious thoughts and painful memories. Mindfulness offers a way to anchor ourselves in the present, to reconnect with our bodies, and to create a safe space within ourselves where we can observe our thoughts and emotions without being overwhelmed by them.

One of the key benefits of mindfulness for trauma recovery is its ability to help us regulate our emotions. When we practice mindfulness, we learn to observe our emotions with curiosity and compassion, rather than reacting to them impulsively. We learn to recognize the physical sensations associated with different emotions, such as tightness in the chest for anger or a knot in the stomach for anxiety. This awareness allows us to respond to our emotions in a more skillful way, choosing healthy coping mechanisms rather than resorting to self-destructive behaviors.

Mindfulness also helps us to cultivate a sense of self-compassion. Trauma often leaves us feeling ashamed, guilty, or unworthy. We may blame ourselves for what happened or believe that we are somehow flawed or broken. Mindfulness teaches us to be kind and gentle with ourselves, to acknowledge our pain and suffering without judgment. It helps us to develop a more loving and accepting relationship with ourselves, which is essential for healing.

The practice of mindfulness is simple, yet profound. It can be as easy as taking a few deep breaths, paying attention to the sensations of your breath as it enters and leaves your body. It can involve focusing on the sounds around you, the feeling of your feet on the ground, or the taste of your food. It can also involve more formal practices like meditation, where you sit quietly and observe your thoughts and emotions without getting caught up in them.

The key to mindfulness is to approach it with an open mind and a willingness to experiment. There is no right or wrong way to practice mindfulness. What works for one person may not work for another. The most important thing is to find practices that resonate with you and to incorporate them into your daily life.

Consider the story of Sarah, a woman who struggled with anxiety and flashbacks after a traumatic car accident. She found it difficult to sleep, her mind racing with thoughts of the accident and fears for the future. She began practicing mindfulness meditation, starting with just a few minutes each day. At first, she found it difficult to quiet her mind, but with practice, she began to notice a shift. She became more aware of her thoughts and emotions, but she was less reactive to them. She was able to observe her anxiety without getting caught up in it. Over time, her sleep improved, her flashbacks subsided, and she felt a greater sense of calm and well-being.

Mindfulness is not a magic bullet, and it won't erase the pain of the past. But it can offer a powerful tool for healing, a way to anchor ourselves in the present moment, to cultivate self-compassion, and to find peace amidst the storm.

Being Present: Anchoring Yourself in the Now

"The present moment is the only reality."

Trauma can fracture our sense of time, leaving us trapped in the past or consumed by fears of the future. It can create a disorienting whirlwind where intrusive thoughts and memories reign supreme, robbing us of the peace and serenity that reside in the present moment. Yet, amidst this turbulence, there exists a powerful anchor, a sanctuary of stillness that can ground us and foster healing: mindfulness.

Mindfulness, often described as the practice of paying non-judgmental attention to the present moment, offers a lifeline for those grappling with the aftermath of trauma. It's not about erasing the past or denying its impact but rather about cultivating a new relationship with our experiences. It's about learning to observe our thoughts and emotions without getting swept away by them, to be fully present in the here and now, and to reclaim our power from the clutches of the past.

Scientific research supports the profound impact of mindfulness on trauma recovery. Studies have shown that mindfulness practices can significantly reduce symptoms of post-traumatic stress disorder (PTSD), anxiety, and depression. It can also enhance emotional regulation, improve sleep, and foster a greater sense of well-being. For those who have experienced trauma, mindfulness can be a transformative tool, offering a pathway to healing and resilience.

At its core, mindfulness is about cultivating awareness. It's about paying attention to the present moment, not with a critical or analytical mind, but with an open, curious, and accepting heart. It's about noticing the sensations in our bodies, the thoughts that arise in our minds, and the emotions that flicker across our hearts. By cultivating this awareness, we create space between ourselves and our experiences, allowing us to respond to them with greater clarity and wisdom.

For those who have experienced trauma, this space can be a lifesaver. It allows us to observe our intrusive thoughts and memories without getting caught up in them. Instead of being swept away by a wave of anxiety or a flashback to a traumatic event, we can simply notice the thought or memory, acknowledge its presence, and then gently let it go. This doesn't mean that the thoughts or memories disappear entirely, but it does mean that we are no longer held captive by them.

Mindfulness also helps us to ground ourselves in the present moment. Trauma can often leave us feeling ungrounded and disconnected from our bodies. We may find ourselves ruminating on the past or worrying about the future, our minds racing with anxious thoughts and painful memories. By focusing our attention on the present moment, we can anchor ourselves in the here and now, finding a sense of stability and peace amidst the chaos.

One simple way to practice mindfulness is to focus on your breath. Take a few deep breaths, feeling the rise and fall of your chest, the sensation of the air entering and leaving your nostrils. Notice the quality of your breath – is it shallow or deep, smooth or ragged? By anchoring your attention on your breath, you can bring yourself back to the present moment and create a sense of calm and relaxation.

Another way to practice mindfulness is to engage your senses. Take a moment to notice the sights, sounds, smells, tastes, and textures around you. What do you see? What do you hear? What do you smell? By engaging your senses, you can fully immerse yourself in the present moment, grounding yourself in the here and now.

Mindfulness is not a quick fix, nor is it a substitute for professional help. But it can be a valuable tool in the healing process, offering a way to manage the symptoms of trauma, to cultivate self-compassion, and to find peace and serenity in the present moment. It's a practice that can be incorporated into daily life, whether through formal meditation, mindful movement, or simply taking a few moments to pause and breathe.

Mindful Practices for Trauma Recovery

"You can't stop the waves, but you can learn to surf."

The journey of healing from trauma is often likened to navigating a turbulent sea. The waves of memories, emotions, and sensations can feel overwhelming, threatening to capsize us at any moment. But mindfulness offers a surfboard, a tool to ride those waves, to find balance amidst the chaos, and to eventually reach the shore of peace and well-being.

Mindful practices are not about erasing the past or numbing the pain. They are about cultivating a new relationship with our experiences, a relationship based on awareness, acceptance, and compassion. They are about learning to be present with our pain, to observe it without judgment, and to allow it to move through us without becoming overwhelmed by it.

One of the most fundamental mindful practices is mindful breathing. It's a simple yet powerful tool that can be used anytime, anywhere, to anchor ourselves in the present moment and to calm our nervous system. Here's how to practice mindful breathing:

1. Find a comfortable position, either sitting or lying down.
2. Close your eyes or soften your gaze.
3. Bring your attention to your breath, noticing the sensation of the air entering and leaving your nostrils or the rise and fall of your abdomen.
4. If your mind wanders, which it inevitably will, gently bring your attention back to your breath.

5. Continue for a few minutes, simply observing your breath without trying to change it.

Mindful breathing can be practiced for as little as a few minutes or as long as you like. It's a portable practice that you can take with you wherever you go, offering a quick and easy way to de-stress and reconnect with yourself.

Another powerful mindful practice is the body scan. This involves systematically bringing awareness to different parts of your body, noticing any sensations that are present without judgment. Here's how to practice a body scan:

1. Lie down or sit comfortably in a chair.//
2. Close your eyes or soften your gaze.
3. Start by bringing your attention to your toes. Notice any sensations you feel, such as tingling, warmth, or coolness.

4. Slowly move your attention up your body, noticing the sensations in your feet, ankles, calves, knees, thighs, hips, and so on.

5. Continue scanning your body, paying attention to each part in turn, until you reach the top of your head.

6. If your mind wanders, gently bring your attention back to the body part you were focusing on.

A body scan can help you to reconnect with your body and to become more aware of the physical manifestations of your emotions. It can also help you to release tension and promote relaxation.

Mindful walking is another practice that can be easily integrated into daily life. It involves paying attention to the sensations of walking, noticing the movement of your feet, the feeling of the ground beneath you, and the rhythm of your breath. You can practice mindful walking anywhere, whether it's on a nature trail, a city street, or even in your own home.

Here are some tips for incorporating mindfulness into your daily life:

- **Start small:** Begin with just a few minutes of mindful practice each day, gradually increasing the duration as you become more comfortable.

- **Set reminders:** Use a timer or an app to remind yourself to practice mindfulness throughout the day.

- **Find a quiet space:** Choose a peaceful environment where you won't be disturbed.

- **Be patient:** Mindfulness takes practice. Don't get discouraged if your mind wanders – simply bring your attention back to the present moment.

- **Be kind to yourself:** Approach your practice with self-compassion. There is no right or wrong way to practice mindfulness.

Self-Reflection Questions:

1. In what areas of my life do I feel most disconnected from the present moment? What thoughts, emotions, or behaviors pull me away from the here and now?

2. How often do I find myself ruminating on the past or worrying about the future? What triggers these thought patterns?

3. How does my body feel when I am stressed or triggered? What physical sensations do I experience?

4. What mindful practices do I feel most drawn to? Which ones resonate with me on a personal level?

5. What are my intentions for incorporating mindfulness into my life? What do I hope to gain from this practice?

Transformative Exercises:

1. **Mindful Breathing Practice:** Set a timer for five minutes. Find a comfortable seated

position, close your eyes, and bring your attention to your breath. Notice the sensation of the air entering and leaving your nostrils or the rise and fall of your abdomen. If your mind wanders, gently guide it back to your breath. Repeat this practice daily, gradually increasing the duration as you feel comfortable.

2. **Body Scan Meditation:** Lie down or sit comfortably in a chair. Close your eyes and begin to scan your body from head to toe, noticing any sensations that arise. Pay attention to areas of tension, pain, or discomfort, as well as areas of ease and relaxation. As you scan your body, send each part a message of kindness and acceptance.

3. **Mindful Walking:** Take a walk in nature or a quiet environment. As you walk, pay attention to the sensations of your feet hitting the ground, the feeling of the air on your skin, and the sights and sounds around you. Notice

each step you take, fully immersing yourself in the experience of walking.

4. **Mindful Eating:** Choose a meal or snack to eat mindfully. Before you begin, take a few deep breaths and bring your awareness to the present moment. As you eat, pay attention to the taste, texture, and smell of the food. Notice how it feels in your mouth and how your body reacts to it. Avoid distractions like TV or phones, and savor each bite.

5. **Mindful Journaling:** Set aside some time each day to write in a journal. Reflect on your experiences, thoughts, and emotions without judgment. Write down any insights or observations that arise during your mindfulness practice. This can help you to deepen your understanding of yourself and your relationship to your experiences.

Chapter 5: Cultivating Self-Compassion

"Love yourself first and everything else falls into line. You really have to love yourself to get anything done in this world." – Lucille Ball

In the labyrinthine journey of healing, where shadows of the past often linger, a gentle light emerges to guide us forward: self-compassion. This transformative practice, often misunderstood as self-indulgence or weakness, is in fact a profound act of courage and a cornerstone of resilience. It's a radical departure from the harsh inner critic that often berates us for our perceived flaws and shortcomings, and a loving embrace of our shared humanity.

Self-compassion is not about ignoring our pain or pretending that everything is okay. It's about acknowledging our suffering with kindness and understanding, offering ourselves the same warmth and care we would extend to a dear friend in need. It's about recognizing that we are not perfect, that we will make mistakes and experience setbacks, and that this is simply part of the human experience.

The concept of self-compassion, as defined by Dr. Kristin Neff, a leading researcher in the field, consists of three core components: self-kindness, common humanity, and mindfulness. Self-kindness involves treating ourselves with gentleness and understanding, rather than harsh self-judgment. Common humanity recognizes that suffering is a universal human experience, that we are not alone in our struggles. Mindfulness involves observing our thoughts and emotions without judgment, allowing us to be present with our experience without getting overwhelmed by it.

The benefits of self-compassion are far-reaching. Research has shown that self-compassion can reduce anxiety, depression, and stress, while increasing happiness, resilience, and overall well-being. It can also enhance our relationships, improve our body image, and even boost our motivation and performance. For those who have experienced trauma, self-compassion can be a particularly powerful tool for healing, offering a safe haven from the storms of self-blame and shame.

One of the key benefits of self-compassion is that it helps us to break free from the cycle of self-criticism and negative self-talk. When we are caught in this cycle, we tend to magnify our flaws and minimize our strengths. We become our own worst enemies, constantly berating ourselves for our perceived shortcomings. This harsh inner critic can be relentless, chipping away at our self-esteem and leaving us feeling unworthy and unlovable.

Self-compassion offers an antidote to this negativity. It allows us to see ourselves with greater clarity and kindness, recognizing that we are not defined by our mistakes or our imperfections. It helps us to develop a more balanced and realistic view of ourselves, acknowledging both our strengths and our weaknesses.

Another important benefit of self-compassion is that it fosters resilience in the face of adversity. When we are kind and understanding towards ourselves, we are better able to cope with challenges and setbacks. We are less likely to get bogged down by self-blame and more likely to bounce back from difficult experiences. This resilience is essential for healing from trauma, as it allows us to face our pain with courage and determination, rather than being overwhelmed by it.

Self-compassion can also enhance our relationships with others. When we are kind and understanding towards ourselves, we are more likely to extend that same kindness and understanding to others. We are less likely to judge or criticize others, and more likely to offer empathy and support. This can lead to deeper, more meaningful connections with the people around us.

Cultivating self-compassion is a journey, not a destination. It takes time, patience, and practice. But with each step we take, we move closer to a place of greater self-acceptance, love, and inner peace. We discover that we are worthy of kindness, not just from others, but also from ourselves.

Imagine a world where we treat ourselves with the same compassion we would offer to a dear friend. A world where we speak to ourselves with kindness, where we forgive ourselves for our mistakes, and where we embrace our imperfections with love and acceptance. This is the world that self-compassion invites us to create, both within ourselves and in our relationships with others.

The Antidote to Self-Blame: Befriending Yourself

"Be kind to yourself. It's where all change begins."

In the aftermath of trauma, the mind often becomes a battleground. The echoes of the past reverberate, triggering a cascade of negative self-beliefs. We replay the events, scrutinizing our every action, dissecting our every word, searching for the fatal flaw that led to our suffering. We blame ourselves for not being strong enough, smart enough, or worthy enough. We tell ourselves that we are damaged, broken, or unlovable. This relentless self-blame, while a common response to trauma, is a poison that hinders our healing.

Research has shown that self-blame is a major risk factor for developing post-traumatic stress disorder (PTSD) and other mental health conditions. It can also impede recovery, prolonging the cycle of suffering and preventing us from moving forward. When we are caught in the grip of self-blame, we become trapped in a self-perpetuating cycle of shame, guilt, and self-loathing.

But there is an antidote to this poison: self-compassion. Self-compassion is not about self-indulgence or denial of responsibility. It's about treating ourselves with the same kindness, care, and understanding that we would offer to a dear friend who is struggling. It's about recognizing that we are human, imperfect, and vulnerable, and that making mistakes or experiencing hardship does not diminish our worth.

When we practice self-compassion, we challenge the negative self-beliefs that can hinder our healing. We recognize that we are not to blame for the trauma we experienced, that we did the best we could with the resources we had at the time. We learn to differentiate between responsibility and blame, acknowledging that while we may have made choices that contributed to our situation, we are not responsible for the actions of others.

Self-compassion also involves cultivating a sense of common humanity. We recognize that suffering is a universal human experience, that we are not alone in our pain. We understand that everyone makes mistakes, experiences setbacks, and faces challenges. This recognition can help us to feel less isolated and more connected to others, fostering a sense of belonging and support.

Mindfulness is another key component of self-compassion. It involves paying attention to our thoughts and emotions without judgment, simply observing them as they arise and pass away. When we practice mindfulness, we create space between ourselves and our thoughts, allowing us to see them as mental events rather than absolute truths. This can help us to challenge negative self-beliefs and to cultivate a more balanced and realistic view of ourselves.

Forgiveness, both of ourselves and others, is also an integral part of self-compassion. When we forgive ourselves, we acknowledge that we are human and capable of making mistakes. We release ourselves from the burden of guilt and shame, allowing us to move forward with greater ease and grace. When we forgive others, we release the anger and resentment that keep us tethered to the past, opening ourselves up to the possibility of healing and reconciliation.

The practice of self-compassion is not a one-time event; it's an ongoing process. It requires patience, perseverance, and a willingness to confront our own inner critic. But the rewards are immeasurable. When we cultivate self-compassion, we create a safe and supportive inner environment where healing can flourish. We learn to treat ourselves with kindness and understanding, to forgive ourselves for our mistakes, and to embrace our imperfections with love and acceptance.

Practices for Self-Care and Nurturing

"Self-care is giving the world the best of you, instead of what's left of you." – Katie Reed

In the pursuit of healing what we can't forget, self-care is not a luxury; it's a necessity. It's the foundation upon which we rebuild our lives, the nourishment we provide to our wounded hearts and weary souls. It's the oxygen mask we secure for ourselves before assisting others, ensuring that we have the strength and resilience to navigate the turbulent waters of recovery.

Self-care is not a one-size-fits-all prescription, but rather a personalized journey of discovery and experimentation. It's about tuning into our unique needs and finding practices that nourish our minds, bodies, and spirits. It's about prioritizing our well-being, not as an act of selfishness, but as a fundamental act of self-love.

Emotional self-care is about tending to our inner landscape, acknowledging and validating our feelings, and finding healthy outlets for expression. It might involve journaling, talking to a trusted friend or therapist, engaging in creative activities, or simply allowing ourselves to cry or scream. It's about giving ourselves permission to feel the full spectrum of our emotions, without judgment or suppression.

Physical self-care is about honoring our bodies, recognizing them as sacred vessels that deserve our love and attention. It involves nourishing ourselves with wholesome foods, moving our bodies in ways that feel good, and getting enough rest and sleep. It's about listening to our bodies' signals and responding to their needs with compassion and care.

Spiritual self-care is about connecting with something larger than ourselves, whether it's nature, a higher power, or a sense of universal interconnectedness. It can involve practices like meditation, prayer, spending time in nature, or engaging in activities that bring us joy and inspiration. It's about nurturing our souls, finding meaning and purpose in our lives, and cultivating a sense of peace and gratitude.

Developing a self-care routine that prioritizes our needs is essential for healing and well-being. It's about creating a rhythm of nourishment and restoration, a sanctuary where we can recharge and reconnect with ourselves. This routine might include daily practices like meditation, journaling, or exercise, as well as weekly or monthly rituals like getting a massage, taking a nature walk, or spending time with loved ones.

One of the most important aspects of self-care is learning to say no. In a world that often glorifies busyness and productivity, it can be difficult to set boundaries and prioritize our own needs. But saying no to commitments that drain our energy or don't align with our values is a crucial act of self-preservation. It allows us to protect our time and energy for the things that truly matter.

Another essential aspect of self-care is learning to be present in the moment. Mindfulness practices, such as meditation, yoga, or simply taking a few deep breaths, can help us to anchor ourselves in the here and now, reducing stress and promoting relaxation. When we are fully present, we are more likely to make choices that are aligned with our values and that support our well-being.

Self-care is not a one-time event; it's an ongoing practice, a lifelong commitment to ourselves. It's about creating a sustainable rhythm of nourishment and restoration that allows us to thrive, not just survive. It's about recognizing that our well-being is not a luxury, but a necessity, a fundamental human right.

The journey to healing what we can't forget is a deeply personal one. There is no one-size-fits-all approach. But self-care is a universal language, a common thread that weaves through all healing journeys. It's a reminder that we are worthy of love, care, and compassion, not just from others, but also from ourselves.

As you embark on your own healing journey, remember to be kind to yourself. Listen to your body, honor your emotions, and nourish your spirit. Create a self-care routine that prioritizes your needs and supports your well-being. And above all, remember that self-care is not selfish. It's an act of radical self-love, a gift you give yourself, and a pathway to a more vibrant, joyful, and fulfilling life.

Self-Reflection Questions:

1. How do I typically talk to myself when I make a mistake or face a challenge? Is my inner dialogue kind and supportive, or harsh and critical?

2. What are some common negative self-beliefs that I hold about myself? Where did these beliefs originate?

3. How does self-criticism affect my emotional and physical well-being? What are the consequences of being harsh with myself?

4. What would it feel like to treat myself with the same kindness and understanding that I offer to others?

5. What are some small steps I can take today to cultivate more self-compassion in my life?

Transformative Exercises:

1. **Self-Compassion Break:** When you notice yourself feeling stressed, overwhelmed, or self-critical, take a moment to pause and acknowledge your feelings. Place your hands on your heart or stomach, and say to yourself, "This is a moment of suffering. May I be kind to myself. May I give myself the compassion I need." Repeat this phrase several times, focusing on the sensations of warmth and comfort in your body.

2. **Loving-Kindness Meditation:** Find a comfortable seated position and close your eyes. Begin by sending feelings of love and kindness to yourself, repeating phrases like "May I be happy. May I be healthy. May I be safe. May I be at peace." Then, extend these wishes to loved ones, acquaintances, and even those you find difficult. Finally, expand your circle of compassion to include all beings, repeating the phrase "May all beings be

happy. May all beings be healthy. May all beings be safe. May all beings be at peace."

3. **Self-Compassionate Letter:** Write a letter to yourself from the perspective of a loving and supportive friend. Acknowledge your struggles, validate your emotions, and offer words of encouragement and support. Remind yourself of your strengths, your resilience, and your inherent worthiness of love and compassion.

4. **Challenging Negative Self-Talk:** When you notice yourself engaging in negative self-talk, pause and ask yourself, "Would I speak to a friend this way?" If the answer is no, then challenge the negative thought and replace it with a more compassionate and realistic one.

5. **Acts of Kindness Towards Yourself:** Make a list of small, enjoyable activities that you can do for yourself each day. These could include taking a warm bath, reading a book, listening to music, spending time in nature, or

simply taking a few minutes to relax and recharge. By prioritizing your own needs and well-being, you are demonstrating self-compassion in action.

Chapter 6: Building Resilience: The Art of Bouncing Back

"Resilience is accepting your new reality, even if it's less good than the one you had before. You can fight it, you can do nothing but scream about what you've lost, or you can accept it and try to put together something good." – Elizabeth Edwards

In the face of adversity, the human spirit has an extraordinary capacity to bend without breaking, to adapt, to overcome, and to emerge stronger than before. This remarkable ability is known as resilience, the art of bouncing back from life's inevitable challenges and setbacks. For those who have endured trauma, building resilience is not just a desirable trait; it's a vital component of healing and recovery.

Resilience is not about ignoring or denying the pain of trauma. It's not about pretending that everything is okay when it's not. It's about acknowledging the reality of our experiences, while also recognizing our inherent strength and capacity for growth. It's about developing the inner resources and coping mechanisms that allow us to weather the storms of life, to adapt to change, and to find meaning and purpose in the face of adversity.

Research has shown that resilience is not a fixed trait, but rather a skill that can be learned and developed over time. While some individuals may naturally possess a greater capacity for resilience, everyone can learn to cultivate this quality through practice and intention. In fact, studies have shown that individuals who have experienced trauma can actually develop greater resilience than those who have not, as they learn to adapt and overcome adversity.

Building resilience is a multifaceted process, involving a combination of internal and external factors. It requires developing a strong sense of self-efficacy, the belief in our ability to cope with challenges and achieve our goals. It also involves cultivating healthy coping mechanisms, such as mindfulness, exercise, social support, and seeking professional help when needed.

One of the key components of resilience is the ability to regulate our emotions. When we are faced with stress or adversity, our emotions can easily become overwhelming, leading to impulsive reactions and unhealthy coping mechanisms. By learning to identify and manage our emotions in a healthy way, we can reduce their intensity and duration, allowing us to respond to challenges with greater clarity and composure.

Another important aspect of resilience is the ability to reframe our experiences. Trauma can often leave us feeling like victims, powerless in the face of overwhelming circumstances. But by reframing our experiences, we can shift our perspective from victimhood to empowerment. We can see ourselves not as passive recipients of fate, but as active agents in our own lives, capable of making choices and taking action.

This reframing process often involves challenging negative self-beliefs and replacing them with more positive and empowering ones. It might involve recognizing that we are not responsible for the trauma that happened to us, but we are responsible for how we respond to it. It might involve acknowledging our strengths and resources, and using them to overcome adversity and create a better future for ourselves.

Building resilience also involves cultivating a strong sense of social support. Having a network of supportive friends, family members, or professionals can provide us with the emotional and practical support we need to navigate challenging times. It can also help us to feel less isolated and more connected to others, fostering a sense of belonging and community.

Another crucial aspect of resilience is the ability to find meaning and purpose in the face of adversity. Trauma can often shatter our sense of meaning, leaving us feeling lost and adrift. But by seeking out meaning and purpose, we can find a new sense of direction and motivation. This might involve volunteering our time, pursuing a passion, or simply focusing on our relationships and personal growth.

Developing Inner Strength: Tools for Coping

"The oak fought the wind and was broken, the willow bent when it must and survived." – Robert Jordan

Resilience, the ability to bounce back from adversity, is not a magical trait bestowed upon a select few. It's a skill, a muscle that can be strengthened and honed with practice and intention. It's the inner strength we cultivate to weather life's storms, the tools we gather to navigate the turbulent waters of trauma.

The human capacity for resilience is nothing short of remarkable. Studies have shown that individuals who have experienced trauma can not only recover but also thrive in the aftermath. They develop a heightened sense of gratitude, a deeper appreciation for life, and a newfound sense of purpose and meaning. This phenomenon, known as post-traumatic growth, is a testament to the power of the human spirit to adapt, overcome, and even flourish in the face of adversity.

But building resilience is not a passive process. It requires active engagement and a willingness to explore different coping mechanisms. It's about creating a personalized "toolkit" of strategies that we can draw upon when faced with challenges, setbacks, or triggers. This toolkit can include a wide range of practices, from mindfulness and relaxation techniques to creative expression and social connection.

One of the most effective tools for managing stress and anxiety is mindfulness. By bringing our attention to the present moment, we can interrupt the cycle of rumination and worry that often accompanies trauma. Mindfulness practices, such as meditation, yoga, or simply taking a few deep breaths, can help us to calm our nervous system, reduce our stress levels, and cultivate a sense of inner peace.

Another powerful coping mechanism is physical activity. Exercise has been shown to have a profound impact on mental health, reducing symptoms of anxiety and depression, improving mood, and boosting self-esteem. Whether it's a brisk walk in nature, a yoga class, or a high-intensity workout, finding ways to move our bodies can be a powerful antidote to stress and trauma.

Creative expression can also be a transformative tool for healing. Writing, painting, drawing, music, dance, and other forms of creative expression offer a safe and healthy outlet for emotions that may be difficult to put into words. They can help us to process our experiences, make sense of our feelings, and find new meaning and purpose in the aftermath of trauma.

Social connection is another vital component of resilience. Having a strong support network of friends, family members, or professionals can provide us with the emotional and practical support we need to navigate challenging times. Sharing our stories with others who understand our experiences can help us to feel less alone and more connected to the human community.

In addition to these core practices, there are countless other tools that can be added to our resilience toolkit. Some people find solace in nature, spending time outdoors to reconnect with the natural world and to find a sense of peace and tranquility. Others find comfort in spirituality or religion, drawing strength from their faith and community. Still, others find healing in therapy, working with a trained professional to process their trauma and develop healthy coping mechanisms.

The key is to experiment and find the practices that work best for you. What works for one person may not work for another. The most important thing is to be open to trying new things and to be patient with yourself as you explore different options.

Building resilience is not about becoming invincible or immune to pain. It's about developing the inner resources and coping mechanisms that allow us to face life's challenges with courage, grace, and resilience. It's about acknowledging our vulnerability while also recognizing our strength. It's about learning to bend without breaking, to adapt, to overcome, and to emerge from adversity stronger than before.

Post-Traumatic Growth: Finding Meaning in Adversity

"What hurts you, blesses you. Darkness is your candle." – Rumi

The aftermath of trauma can feel like a barren wasteland, a landscape stripped of color and joy. The pain, the loss, the shattered sense of self – it can all seem insurmountable. But what if, amidst the wreckage, there were seeds of transformation waiting to sprout? What if, through the very act of healing, we could not only recover but actually thrive? This is the promise of post-traumatic growth, a phenomenon that reveals the extraordinary capacity of the human spirit to find meaning and purpose in the face of adversity.

Post-traumatic growth (PTG) is not a magical cure-all, nor is it a denial of the pain and suffering caused by trauma. It's a testament to the resilience of the human spirit, the ability to adapt, evolve, and even flourish in the wake of adversity. It's a reminder that even in the darkest of times, there is potential for growth, healing, and transformation.

Research suggests that a significant proportion of individuals who experience trauma go on to experience PTG. This growth manifests in various ways, including a greater appreciation for life, stronger relationships, a heightened sense of personal strength, and a deeper sense of meaning and purpose. It's a paradoxical phenomenon, where the very experience that threatened to break us becomes the catalyst for our greatest transformation.

The journey towards PTG is not a linear one. It's a winding path filled with twists and turns, setbacks and breakthroughs. It requires courage, perseverance, and a willingness to confront our pain head-on. But for those who embark on this journey, the rewards can be profound.

Consider the story of Malala Yousafzai, a young Pakistani activist who was shot in the head by the Taliban for advocating for girls' education. In the aftermath of this horrific event, Malala could have easily succumbed to fear and despair. But instead, she emerged from her ordeal with a renewed sense of purpose and a determination to fight for the rights of others. Her pain became a source of inspiration, fueling her activism and transforming her into a global symbol of courage and resilience.

The story of Christopher Reeve, the actor best known for his portrayal of Superman, offers another inspiring example of PTG. After a devastating horse-riding accident left him paralyzed from the neck down, Reeve could have easily given up on life. But instead, he chose to focus on the things he could still do, becoming an advocate for spinal cord research and a beacon of hope for others facing similar challenges. His courage and determination in the face of adversity inspired millions around the world.

These are just two examples of individuals who have experienced post-traumatic growth. There are countless others, from everyday heroes who have overcome adversity to find new meaning and purpose in their lives, to survivors of natural disasters, violence, and illness who have used their experiences to advocate for change and to help others in need.

The path to PTG is not easy, but it is possible. It begins with acknowledging our pain and allowing ourselves to grieve the losses we have experienced. It involves seeking support from loved ones, professionals, or support groups. It requires developing healthy coping mechanisms, such as mindfulness, exercise, and creative expression. And it involves finding ways to reframe our experiences, to see them not as sources of shame or weakness, but as opportunities for growth and transformation.

One powerful way to find meaning in adversity is to focus on helping others. By volunteering our time, skills, or resources, we can shift our focus from our own pain to the needs of others. This can not only provide us with a sense of purpose and meaning, but it can also help us to connect with others who are also struggling, fostering a sense of community and support.

Another way to find meaning is to explore our creative side. Writing, painting, music, or other forms of creative expression can offer a safe space to process our emotions, to express the inexpressible, and to find beauty in the midst of pain. Creativity can also be a powerful tool for connecting with others and for raising awareness about important issues.

Ultimately, the journey to post-traumatic growth is a deeply personal one. There is no one-size-fits-all approach. But by acknowledging our pain, seeking support, developing healthy coping mechanisms, and finding ways to reframe our experiences, we can transform our wounds into wellsprings of wisdom, resilience, and compassion. We can emerge from the darkness of trauma stronger, wiser, and more connected to ourselves and others.

Self-Reflection Questions:

1. When faced with challenges or setbacks, what are my typical reactions? Do I tend to shut down, become overwhelmed, or try to avoid the situation?

2. What are my strengths and resources that I can draw upon during difficult times? How have I overcome challenges in the past?

3. What are my go-to coping mechanisms for managing stress and anxiety? Are these mechanisms healthy and sustainable?

4. Who are the people in my life who support me and offer me encouragement? How can I strengthen my support network?

5. What are some activities or practices that bring me joy and a sense of meaning? How can I incorporate these into my daily life?

Transformative Exercises:

1. **Resilience Journal:** Create a journal specifically for tracking your resilience journey. Each day, write down one challenge you faced and how you overcame it. Reflect on the strengths and resources you utilized, and any lessons you learned.

2. **Gratitude Practice:** Every day, write down three things you are grateful for. This practice can help shift your focus from negativity to appreciation, fostering a more positive and resilient outlook.

3. **Self-Care Ritual:** Develop a daily self-care routine that includes activities that nourish your mind, body, and spirit. This could include meditation, exercise, reading, spending time in nature, or engaging in a creative hobby.

4. **Connecting with Others:** Reach out to a friend, family member, or support group to share your experiences and feelings. Connecting with others who understand your struggles can provide a sense of comfort and support.

5. **Finding Your Purpose:** Explore activities or causes that give you a sense of meaning and purpose. This could involve volunteering your time, pursuing a passion project, or simply

focusing on your personal growth and development.

Chapter 7: Reconnecting with Your Body

"Your body hears everything your mind says." – Naomi Judd

The human body, a marvel of intricate systems and interconnected pathways, is not merely a vessel for our thoughts and emotions. It is an active participant in our experiences, a living archive of our joys, sorrows, and traumas. When we experience a traumatic event, the impact is not solely psychological; it reverberates through our physical being, leaving an imprint that can manifest as tension, pain, or even illness. Healing what we can't forget, therefore, involves not just addressing the mental and emotional aspects of trauma, but also reconnecting with our bodies and restoring their innate wisdom and resilience.

Research has shown a profound link between trauma and physical health. The Adverse Childhood Experiences (ACE) Study, a landmark investigation, found that individuals who experienced childhood trauma were at significantly higher risk for developing chronic diseases such as heart disease, cancer, and diabetes later in life. This groundbreaking study highlighted the undeniable connection between our emotional experiences and our physical well-being, underscoring the importance of a holistic approach to healing.

But how exactly does trauma affect our bodies? When faced with a threat, real or perceived, our bodies activate a stress response, releasing a flood of hormones such as cortisol and adrenaline. These hormones prepare us to fight, flee, or freeze, priming our bodies for survival. However, when the threat persists or remains unresolved, as is often the case with trauma, this stress response can become chronic, leading to a state of hyperarousal and dysregulation.

Chronic stress can wreak havoc on our bodies, suppressing the immune system, disrupting digestion, and increasing inflammation. It can also lead to changes in the brain, affecting our ability to regulate emotions, form memories, and make decisions. Over time, the cumulative effects of stress can manifest as a range of physical ailments, from chronic pain and fatigue to autoimmune disorders and cardiovascular disease.

But the body is not merely a passive victim of trauma. It also holds the key to our healing. Our bodies are innately wise, constantly communicating with us through sensations, emotions, and intuitive nudges. When we learn to listen to these signals, we can tap into a wellspring of wisdom that can guide us towards recovery.

Reconnecting with our bodies involves cultivating a sense of embodiment, a felt sense of being present in our physical form. It means paying attention to the sensations in our bodies, noticing the subtle cues that tell us when we are stressed, anxious, or triggered. It also means learning to honor our bodies' needs, nourishing ourselves with wholesome foods, moving our bodies in ways that feel good, and getting enough rest and sleep.

One powerful way to reconnect with our bodies is through somatic practices. These practices, which include yoga, tai chi, qigong, and other forms of mindful movement, can help us to release tension, improve flexibility, and cultivate a greater sense of body awareness. They can also help us to process emotions that may be stored in our bodies, allowing us to release them and move towards healing.

Another important aspect of reconnecting with our bodies is learning to regulate our nervous systems. Trauma can leave our nervous systems in a state of hyperarousal, making us feel constantly on edge and easily triggered. Practices such as deep breathing, meditation, and progressive muscle relaxation can help to calm the nervous system and restore a sense of balance and equilibrium.

Touch can also be a powerful tool for healing. Whether it's a warm hug from a loved one, a soothing massage, or simply placing a hand on our hearts, touch can activate the parasympathetic nervous system, which is responsible for rest and relaxation. It can also release oxytocin, a hormone that promotes bonding and connection, helping us to feel safe and secure.

The Mind-Body Connection: Healing from the Inside Out

"Your body is your subconscious mind." – Candace Pert

The human experience is not a duality of mind and body, but an intricate dance of interconnectedness. Our emotions are not merely abstract concepts residing solely in our minds; they are embodied experiences, woven into the very fabric of our physical being. Trauma, with its profound impact on our emotional landscape, leaves an indelible mark on our bodies, etching its presence into our cells, tissues, and organs.

The scientific exploration of this mind-body connection has yielded fascinating insights. Research has shown that emotional trauma can trigger a cascade of physiological responses, altering our brain chemistry, hormone levels, and immune function. This intricate interplay between the mind and body underscores the importance of a holistic approach to healing, one that addresses not just the psychological but also the physical manifestations of trauma.

The Adverse Childhood Experiences (ACE) Study, a groundbreaking investigation into the long-term effects of childhood trauma, revealed a startling correlation between adverse childhood experiences and chronic diseases later in life. Participants who had experienced four or more ACEs were twice as likely to develop heart disease, seven times more likely to become alcoholics, and twelve times more likely to attempt suicide compared to those with no ACEs. This study illuminated the profound and lasting impact of early trauma on physical health, demonstrating that the wounds we carry in our minds can manifest as physical ailments.

But how exactly does emotional trauma translate into physical symptoms? When we experience a traumatic event, our bodies activate a stress response, releasing a flood of hormones such as cortisol and adrenaline. These hormones prepare us to fight, flee, or freeze, priming our bodies for survival. However, when the threat persists or remains unresolved, as is often the case with trauma, this stress response can become chronic, leading to a state of hyperarousal and dysregulation.

Chronic stress can wreak havoc on our bodies, suppressing the immune system, disrupting digestion, and increasing inflammation. It can also lead to changes in the brain, affecting our ability to regulate emotions, form memories, and make decisions. Over time, the cumulative effects of stress can manifest as a wide range of physical ailments, including chronic pain, fatigue, headaches, digestive problems, insomnia, autoimmune disorders, and even cardiovascular disease.

But the body is not merely a passive victim of trauma. It also holds a profound wisdom, a language of sensations and signals that can guide us towards healing. This "body wisdom" is often subtle, whispered in the language of muscle tension, gut feelings, or a racing heart. It's the intuitive knowing that something is wrong, even when our minds can't quite articulate it.

By tuning into our bodies, we can access a wealth of information about our emotional state. We can learn to recognize the physical manifestations of anxiety, such as a tight chest or shallow breathing. We can identify the subtle signs of depression, such as fatigue or a lack of motivation. We can even sense the lingering effects of past traumas, held in the body as tension or pain.

This embodied awareness is not just about identifying symptoms; it's about listening to the stories our bodies hold. It's about recognizing that our bodies are not separate from our minds, but rather an integral part of our whole being. By honoring the wisdom of our bodies, we can gain valuable insights into our emotional landscape, allowing us to address the root causes of our suffering and move towards healing.

The journey to healing from the inside out involves developing a deeper relationship with our bodies. It means learning to listen to their whispers, to honor their needs, and to trust their wisdom. It involves cultivating practices that nourish our bodies, such as yoga, meditation, dance, or simply spending time in nature. It also means being mindful of our thoughts and emotions, recognizing how they impact our physical well-being.

As we reconnect with our bodies, we begin to see them not as adversaries but as allies in our healing journey. We discover that our bodies are not just repositories of pain, but also wellsprings of resilience, strength, and vitality. By honoring the mind-body connection, we open ourselves up to a deeper level of healing, one that addresses not just the symptoms but also the root causes of our suffering.

Somatic Practices for Trauma Release

"Trauma is not what happens to us, but what we hold inside in the absence of an empathetic witness." – Peter A. Levine

The body, often overlooked in the traditional talk-therapy approach to healing, is a profound reservoir of wisdom and resilience. It holds the imprints of our experiences, both joyful and painful, and offers a unique pathway to releasing the trapped energy of trauma. Somatic practices, a diverse array of body-centered techniques, tap into this innate wisdom, inviting us to reconnect with our physical selves and unlock the body's inherent capacity for healing.

These practices are not about bypassing or denying the emotional aspects of trauma. Rather, they recognize the interconnectedness of mind and body, acknowledging that our emotions are not merely abstract concepts but embodied experiences. By engaging with our bodies through movement, breath, and touch, we can access and release the emotional energy that has become stuck, allowing us to heal from the inside out.

One of the most well-known somatic practices is yoga. While often associated with physical fitness, yoga is also a powerful tool for emotional and spiritual well-being. The gentle stretches, twists, and inversions of yoga can help to release tension, improve circulation, and promote relaxation. But beyond the physical benefits, yoga also encourages us to tune into our bodies, to notice sensations, and to cultivate a sense of present-moment awareness. This mindful approach can be particularly helpful for those who have experienced trauma, as it allows us to reconnect with our bodies in a safe and supportive way.

Tai chi, a graceful martial art that originated in China, is another somatic practice that can aid in trauma recovery. With its slow, flowing movements and emphasis on deep breathing, tai chi can help to calm the nervous system, reduce stress, and improve balance and coordination. The meditative aspect of tai chi can also be helpful for cultivating mindfulness and self-awareness, allowing us to observe our thoughts and emotions without judgment.

Qigong, a Chinese practice that combines movement, meditation, and breathwork, is another valuable tool for healing trauma. Qigong exercises, which often involve gentle movements and visualizations, can help to release blocked energy, improve circulation, and promote relaxation. Some qigong practices specifically target the release of trauma, such as Trauma Releasing Exercises (TRE), which involve a series of involuntary muscle tremors that can help to discharge pent-up stress and tension.

In addition to these established practices, there are countless other somatic techniques that can be incorporated into daily life. Here are a few simple exercises that you can try:

1. **Grounding:** Stand with your feet hip-width apart and your knees slightly bent. Feel the soles of your feet connecting with the ground, noticing the sensations of pressure and support. Imagine roots growing down from your feet, anchoring you to the earth. This simple practice can help to bring you back to the present moment and to feel more grounded and centered.

2. **Orienting:** Look around your surroundings, noticing the colors, shapes, and textures. Listen to the sounds around you, the hum of the refrigerator, the chirping of birds, the rustling of leaves. Notice the smells in the air, the scent of coffee, the fragrance of flowers,

the smell of rain. By engaging your senses, you can anchor yourself in the present moment and shift your focus away from intrusive thoughts or memories.

3. **Pendulation:** Notice the natural rhythm of your breath, the rise and fall of your chest, the expansion and contraction of your abdomen. Allow yourself to follow this rhythm, letting your breath guide you into a state of relaxation. This simple practice can help to calm your nervous system and reduce anxiety.

4. **Self-Touch:** Place your hand on your heart and take a few deep breaths. Notice the warmth of your hand and the gentle beating of your heart. This self-soothing gesture can help to activate the parasympathetic nervous system, promoting relaxation and reducing stress.

These are just a few examples of somatic practices that can aid in trauma recovery. It's important to find practices that resonate with you and to experiment with different approaches. The key is to listen to your body, to honor its wisdom, and to trust its innate capacity for healing.

Self-Reflection Questions:

1. How often do I tune into my body and its sensations throughout the day? Do I tend to ignore or disconnect from my physical self?

2. What physical sensations do I experience when I am feeling stressed, anxious, or triggered? Where in my body do I hold tension?

3. Have I ever noticed a connection between my emotional state and my physical health? If so, how have they influenced each other?

4. What types of movement or physical activity do I enjoy? How can I incorporate more of these activities into my daily routine?

5. What are some ways I can practice self-care for my body, such as nourishing it with healthy food, getting enough rest, or seeking

professional support for any physical ailments?

Transformative Exercises:

1. **Body Scan Meditation:** Find a quiet space and lie down or sit comfortably. Close your eyes and bring your attention to each part of your body, starting with your toes and gradually moving up to your head. Notice any sensations you feel, such as warmth, coolness, tingling, or tension. Simply observe these sensations without judgment, allowing yourself to fully experience them.

2. **Mindful Movement:** Choose a form of movement that you enjoy, such as yoga, tai chi, dancing, or walking. As you move, pay attention to the sensations in your body, the rhythm of your breath, and the way your body feels in space. Focus on the present moment, letting go of any thoughts or worries that may arise.

3. **Breath Awareness:** Set aside a few minutes each day to simply sit and observe your breath. Notice the rise and fall of your chest or abdomen, the sensation of the air entering and leaving your nostrils. If your mind wanders, gently bring it back to your breath. This simple practice can help to calm your nervous system and reduce stress.

4. **Self-Massage:** Using your hands, gently massage different parts of your body, such as your shoulders, neck, hands, or feet. Pay attention to any areas of tension and use slow, deliberate strokes to release them. You can also use essential oils or aromatherapy to enhance the experience.

5. **Sensory Exploration:** Take a moment to engage your senses fully. Notice the sights, sounds, smells, tastes, and textures around you. Pay attention to the feeling of the sun on your skin, the sound of the birds singing, the taste of your food, the smell of fresh air. This

practice can help you to connect with the present moment and to appreciate the beauty and abundance of the world around you.

Chapter 8: Healing Through Connection

"Alone we can do so little; together we can do so much." – Helen Keller

The journey of healing from trauma is not one to be undertaken alone. In the aftermath of adversity, the instinct to withdraw and isolate can be strong. The weight of our pain, the fear of vulnerability, and the belief that no one could truly understand our experience can all lead us to seek solace in solitude. However, countless stories and studies reveal that true healing often blossoms within the embrace of connection.

The human species is inherently social, wired for connection and belonging. Our brains are designed to thrive in community, seeking out relationships that offer safety, support, and understanding. When we experience trauma, these social bonds can become frayed or broken, leaving us feeling isolated and adrift. But re-establishing these connections, or forging new ones, can be a powerful catalyst for healing.

The Adverse Childhood Experiences (ACE) Study, a groundbreaking investigation into the long-term effects of childhood trauma, revealed a stark reality: the more adverse experiences a person endured, the greater their risk of developing physical and mental health problems later in life. However, the study also highlighted a crucial protective factor: strong social support. Individuals who had a close confidant or someone they could rely on were more likely to overcome adversity and experience resilience. This finding underscores the profound impact of connection on our well-being, especially in the face of trauma.

When we share our stories with others who have walked a similar path, we break the silence and stigma that often surround trauma. We realize that we are not alone in our pain, that there are others who understand what we've been through. This shared experience can be incredibly validating, offering a sense of solace and belonging that can be difficult to find elsewhere.

Support groups, whether in-person or online, can provide a safe and supportive space for individuals to connect with others who have experienced similar traumas. These groups offer a unique opportunity to share stories, offer encouragement, and receive empathy and understanding. They can also provide valuable information and resources, as well as a sense of community and belonging.

But healing through connection is not limited to formal support groups. It can also occur in our everyday interactions with friends, family members, and even strangers. Simply having someone to listen to our stories, validate our feelings, and offer a comforting presence can be incredibly healing. It can help us to feel seen, heard, and understood, reminding us that we are not alone in our struggles.

Moreover, research has shown that helping others can be a powerful way to heal ourselves. When we volunteer our time, skills, or resources to support others, we shift our focus from our own pain to the needs of others. This can not only provide us with a sense of purpose and meaning, but it can also boost our mood, reduce stress, and enhance our overall well-being.

Of course, not all connections are created equal. Some relationships can be toxic, draining our energy and exacerbating our pain. It's important to be mindful of the people we surround ourselves with, choosing those who offer genuine support, encouragement, and respect. This may involve setting boundaries with certain individuals or even distancing ourselves from those who are not supportive of our healing journey.

Building healthy relationships takes time, effort, and vulnerability. It requires us to let down our guard, to trust others with our stories, and to open our hearts to the possibility of connection. But the rewards are immeasurable. When we allow ourselves to be seen and loved for who we truly are, we create the conditions for deep and lasting healing.

The Importance of Safe Relationships: Building a Support Network

"The most beautiful people we have known are those who have known defeat, known suffering, known struggle, known loss, and have found their way out of thedepths. These persons have an appreciation, a sensitivity, and an understanding of life that fills them with compassion, gentleness, and a deep loving concern. Beautiful people do not just happen." – Elisabeth Kübler-Ross

The human experience is, at its core, a relational one. We are wired for connection, for belonging, for the comfort and safety of shared experiences. This innate need for connection is not merely a social nicety; it is a fundamental aspect of our well-being, a cornerstone of our resilience, and a vital component of healing from trauma.

Research has consistently shown the profound impact of social support on our physical and mental health. Studies have found that individuals with strong social connections have lower rates of depression, anxiety, and stress. They also tend to have stronger immune systems, lower blood pressure, and a reduced risk of chronic diseases. For those who have experienced trauma, social support can be a lifeline, offering a safe harbor where they can find solace, understanding, and encouragement on their journey to recovery.

The importance of safe relationships in healing from trauma cannot be overstated. When we experience a traumatic event, our sense of safety and trust in the world can be shattered. We may feel vulnerable, exposed, and afraid to let others in. But it is precisely in these moments of vulnerability that we need connection the most.

Safe relationships provide a space where we can lower our defenses, share our stories, and be truly seen and heard. They offer a sense of belonging, a reminder that we are not alone in our pain. They provide a source of comfort, encouragement, and validation, helping us to rebuild our sense of self-worth and to regain trust in others.

Cultivating healthy relationships is an essential part of the healing journey. It's about seeking out connections that are based on mutual respect, trust, and understanding. It's about surrounding ourselves with people who uplift us, who believe in us, and who support us unconditionally. It's about creating a network of love and support that can sustain us through the ups and downs of life.

Building a support network can take many forms. It might involve reaching out to friends and family members, joining a support group, seeking therapy, or even connecting with online communities of individuals who share similar experiences. The key is to find people who you feel safe and comfortable with, who you can trust with your vulnerabilities, and who can offer you the support and encouragement you need.

One of the most important aspects of building a support network is learning to communicate our needs clearly and honestly. This can be challenging, especially for those who have experienced trauma, as we may have learned to suppress our emotions or to put the needs of others before our own. But by learning to express our needs assertively, we can create healthier and more fulfilling relationships.

Another important aspect of building a support network is reciprocity. Healthy relationships are not one-sided; they involve giving and receiving support. By offering our own support and encouragement to others, we not only strengthen our connections, but we also contribute to the healing of others. This reciprocity can create a virtuous cycle of support and healing, where we both give and receive the love and care we need to thrive.

Seeking out safe, supportive connections is not always easy. It takes courage, vulnerability, and a willingness to step outside of our comfort zones. But the rewards are immeasurable. When we surround ourselves with people who love and support us, we create a fertile ground for healing and growth. We discover that we are not alone in our struggles, that there are others who understand what we've been through, and that together, we can overcome anything.

The journey to healing what we can't forget is a deeply personal one, but it is not a solitary one. By embracing the power of connection, we tap into a wellspring of strength, resilience, and hope. We discover that we are not alone, that we are loved, and that we are capable of healing and thriving.

Finding Your Tribe: Community and Healing

"We are not meant to go through life alone. We need each other." – Leo Buscaglia

The journey of healing from trauma can be a lonely one. The weight of our experiences, the fear of judgment, and the belief that no one could truly understand our pain can all lead to isolation and withdrawal. Yet, emerging research and countless personal accounts reveal that finding our "tribe" – a community of individuals who share our experiences and understand our struggles – can be a transformative force in the healing process.

Human beings are inherently social creatures, wired for connection and belonging. Our brains are designed to thrive in community, seeking out relationships that offer safety, support, and understanding. When we experience trauma, these social bonds can be fractured, leaving us feeling disconnected and alone. But by reconnecting with others, by finding our tribe, we can tap into a powerful source of healing and resilience.

Studies have shown that social support is a critical factor in recovery from trauma. Individuals who have a strong network of supportive relationships are more likely to overcome adversity, experience post-traumatic growth, and achieve a greater sense of well-being. Community provides a safe space where we can share our stories, receive validation and empathy, and learn from the experiences of others. It offers a sense of belonging, a reminder that we are not alone in our struggles.

Support groups, whether in-person or online, can be a lifeline for those who have experienced trauma. These groups offer a confidential and non-judgmental space where individuals can share their experiences, receive support, and learn from others who have walked a similar path. They can provide a sense of community and belonging, as well as valuable information, resources, and coping strategies.

For many, the anonymity and accessibility of online communities can be particularly appealing. These virtual spaces offer a safe haven for individuals who may feel too ashamed or stigmatized to seek help in person. They allow for connection across geographical boundaries, providing access to a diverse range of perspectives and experiences.

But finding your tribe is not limited to formal support groups. It can also involve connecting with friends, family members, or even strangers who have shared similar experiences. It might mean joining a club or organization that aligns with your interests, volunteering your time for a cause you care about, or simply reaching out to others who you feel a connection with.

The key is to find people who understand your experiences, who can offer empathy and support without judgment. These connections can provide a sense of validation, a reminder that you are not alone, and a source of strength and encouragement on your healing journey.

Consider the story of Sarah, a woman who struggled with the aftermath of a sexual assault. She felt ashamed and isolated, convinced that no one could understand what she had been through. She eventually found solace in an online support group for survivors of sexual violence. There, she connected with other women who shared her experiences and understood her pain. Through their shared stories, she found validation, hope, and a renewed sense of empowerment.

Or take the case of David, a war veteran who struggled with PTSD and isolation. He joined a local veterans' group where he connected with other veterans who had experienced similar traumas. Through their shared experiences, he found a sense of camaraderie and belonging that he had been missing. The group provided him with a safe space to talk about his struggles, to receive support, and to learn from others who had successfully navigated the path to recovery.

These stories illustrate the transformative power of community in healing from trauma. By finding our tribe, we tap into a wellspring of strength, resilience, and hope. We discover that we are not alone, that we are loved, and that we are capable of healing and thriving.

If you are struggling with the aftermath of trauma, I encourage you to reach out and find your tribe. There are countless communities and support groups available, both online and in-person. Don't be afraid to ask for help, to share your story, and to connect with others who understand your experiences. Remember, you are not alone.

Self-Reflection Questions:

1. In what ways do I isolate myself when I'm struggling? Do I tend to withdraw from others, avoid social situations, or keep my feelings bottled up?

2. Who are the people in my life who make me feel safe, supported, and understood? How can I nurture and strengthen these relationships?

3. Are there any communities or groups that I could join to connect with others who share similar experiences? What types of communities would be most beneficial for my healing journey?

4. How comfortable am I with vulnerability? Am I open to sharing my story and struggles with others, or do I tend to hold back?

5. What are some ways I can offer support and encouragement to others? How can I contribute to the healing of my community?

Transformative Exercises:

1. **Reach Out:** Identify one person in your life who you trust and feel safe with. Reach out to them and share something you've been

struggling with. Notice how it feels to express your feelings and receive support.

2. **Join a Support Group:** Research and join a support group, either in-person or online, that focuses on your specific type of trauma or life challenge. Share your experiences, listen to the stories of others, and offer support and encouragement.

3. **Volunteer Your Time:** Find a cause or organization that resonates with you and volunteer your time or skills. Helping others can be a powerful way to connect with your community and to find meaning and purpose in your own life.

4. **Practice Vulnerability:** Choose a safe space, such as with a trusted friend or therapist, and share something you've been holding back. Allow yourself to be seen and heard, even if it feels uncomfortable.

5. **Random Acts of Kindness:** Practice small acts of kindness towards others, such as holding a door open, offering a compliment, or helping someone in need. These simple gestures can create a ripple effect of connection and compassion.

Chapter 9: Rewriting Your Story

"We are not the stories we tell ourselves about ourselves." – Brené Brown

The stories we tell ourselves about our lives shape our identities, our beliefs, and our experiences. These narratives, woven from the threads of our memories, emotions, and perceptions, can either empower us or hold us captive. For those who have endured trauma, these stories often become entangled with pain, fear, and self-blame. We may see ourselves as victims, defined by our wounds, forever scarred by the events of the past. But what if we could rewrite these stories? What if we could reclaim our power, redefine our identities, and create a new narrative that reflects our resilience, strength, and capacity for healing?

The concept of narrative therapy, a form of psychotherapy that focuses on the stories we tell ourselves about our lives, offers a powerful tool for healing from trauma. It recognizes that our stories are not fixed or objective truths, but rather subjective interpretations shaped by our experiences, beliefs, and cultural contexts. By examining and challenging these narratives, we can gain new insights, rewrite limiting beliefs, and create a more empowering story for ourselves.

Rewriting our story is not about denying the reality of our experiences or pretending that the pain didn't happen. It's about reframing our perspective, shifting our focus from victimhood to empowerment. It's about recognizing that we are not defined by our traumas, but rather by our resilience, our courage, and our capacity for growth.

One of the first steps in rewriting our story is to identify the dominant narratives that shape our lives. These narratives often stem from our earliest experiences, the messages we received from our parents, caregivers, and society at large. They can be deeply ingrained, influencing our thoughts, feelings, and behaviors in ways we may not even be aware of.

By examining these narratives with curiosity and compassion, we can begin to unravel their hold on us. We can ask ourselves questions like:

- What stories do I tell myself about myself?
- Are these stories empowering or limiting?
- How do these stories affect my life?
- What new stories would I like to tell?

This process of self-inquiry can be challenging, but it is also incredibly liberating. By bringing our unconscious narratives into conscious awareness, we can begin to challenge them and create new, more empowering stories for ourselves.

Reframing our experiences is another crucial step in rewriting our story. Trauma can leave us feeling helpless, powerless, and at the mercy of external forces. But by reframing our experiences, we can shift our perspective from victimhood to agency. We can recognize that even in the face of adversity, we have choices, we have power, and we have the ability to shape our own destinies.

One way to reframe our experiences is to focus on the lessons we have learned from our pain. What have our struggles taught us about ourselves, about others, about the world? How have our experiences made us stronger, wiser, or more compassionate? By focusing on the positive aspects of our experiences, we can begin to see them as opportunities for growth, rather than sources of shame or regret.

Another way to reframe our experiences is to focus on our strengths and resources. Trauma can often leave us feeling weak and vulnerable, but it's important to remember that we are also resilient and resourceful. By identifying our strengths and resources, we can tap into our inner power and use it to overcome adversity and create a better future for ourselves.

Creating a new chapter in our story involves envisioning a future that is free from the constraints of our past traumas. It's about setting goals, making plans, and taking action towards the life we want to live. It's about recognizing that we are not defined by our past, but rather by our hopes, dreams, and aspirations.

This process of envisioning the future can be incredibly empowering. It allows us to shift our focus from what has been to what can be. It gives us a sense of agency and control over our lives, reminding us that we are the authors of our own stories.

Rewriting our story is not about erasing the past or pretending that the pain didn't happen. It's about acknowledging our experiences, learning from our lessons, and choosing to create a new narrative that reflects our resilience, strength, and capacity for healing. It's a journey of self-discovery, a process of transformation, and a testament to the power of the human spirit to overcome adversity and thrive.

Reframing Your Narrative: From Victim to Survivor

"The moment you change your perception, is the moment you rewrite the chemistry of your body." – Bruce Lipton

The aftermath of trauma can leave us feeling trapped in a narrative of victimhood. The echoes of the past reverberate, whispering tales of helplessness, powerlessness, and brokenness. We may see ourselves as forever defined by our wounds, our identities irrevocably shaped by the events that have scarred us. But this narrative, while understandable, is not the only story available to us. Through the transformative power of reframing, we can shift our self-perception, reclaim our agency, and rewrite our narrative from one of victimhood to one of empowerment and resilience.

The stories we tell ourselves about our lives have a profound impact on our well-being. When we identify as victims, we give our power away to the past, allowing it to dictate our present and future. We become trapped in a cycle of self-blame, shame, and despair. But when we reframe our narrative, when we choose to see ourselves as survivors, we reclaim our power and open ourselves up to the possibility of healing and transformation.

Reframing is not about denying the reality of our experiences or minimizing the pain we have endured. It's about shifting our perspective, choosing to focus on our strengths and resilience rather than our wounds. It's about recognizing that we are not defined by what has happened to us, but rather by how we choose to respond to it.

One powerful tool for reframing our narrative is the practice of mindfulness. By bringing our attention to the present moment, we can create space between ourselves and our thoughts, allowing us to observe them without judgment. This awareness can help us to identify the negative self-talk that often accompanies trauma and to challenge the limiting beliefs that keep us trapped in a victim mentality.

When we notice ourselves engaging in negative self-talk, such as "I'm not good enough," "I'm damaged goods," or "I'll never be happy again," we can pause and ask ourselves, "Is this really true? Is this thought serving me?" By questioning our beliefs, we can begin to dismantle the narratives that hold us back.

Another powerful tool for reframing our narrative is gratitude. When we focus on the things we are grateful for, even in the midst of pain and adversity, we shift our perspective from lack to abundance, from despair to hope. Gratitude can help us to see the silver linings in our experiences, the unexpected gifts that emerge from our struggles.

Affirmations can also be helpful in rewriting our story. By repeating positive statements about ourselves and our abilities, we can reprogram our subconscious mind and create new, empowering beliefs. For example, instead of saying, "I'm broken," we can say, "I am healing." Instead of saying, "I'm a victim," we can say, "I am a survivor."

Another transformative practice is journaling. Writing about our experiences can help us to process our emotions, make sense of our thoughts, and gain new insights into our lives. By putting our experiences into words, we can begin to create a new narrative, one that reflects our strength, resilience, and capacity for healing.

It's important to remember that reframing our narrative is not a one-time event; it's an ongoing process. There will be days when the old stories resurface, when the negative self-talk threatens to overwhelm us. But with practice and persistence, we can learn to challenge these thoughts, to reframe our experiences, and to create a new narrative that empowers us to heal and thrive.

The journey from victim to survivor is not an easy one. It requires courage, vulnerability, and a willingness to confront our deepest fears. But the rewards are immeasurable. When we reframe our narrative, we reclaim our power, our agency, and our ability to shape our own destiny. We step out of the shadows of the past and into the light of a brighter future. We become the authors of our own stories, the creators of our own reality.

Creating a New Chapter: Envisioning Your Future

"The best way to predict the future is to create it." – Peter Drucker

The past may be etched in our memories, but it doesn't have to dictate our future. Trauma, while undeniably impactful, doesn't have to be the final chapter in our life story. We have the power to turn the page, to embark on a new chapter filled with hope, healing, and the fulfillment of our deepest aspirations. Envisioning a future free from the constraints of our past traumas is not merely wishful thinking; it's a crucial step in the healing process, a beacon of light guiding us towards a brighter tomorrow.

This process of envisioning the future is not about erasing the past or pretending that the pain didn't happen. It's about acknowledging our experiences, honoring our resilience, and choosing to create a new narrative for our lives. It's about recognizing that we are not defined by our traumas, but rather by our hopes, dreams, and aspirations.

The human mind is a powerful tool for creation. What we focus on expands, and by envisioning a positive future, we set in motion a chain of events that can lead to its manifestation. This is not about magical thinking or denying the challenges that may lie ahead. It's about harnessing the power of our imagination to create a compelling vision that motivates us to take action and move towards our goals.

Setting goals is a crucial step in creating a new chapter in our lives. Goals provide us with direction, focus, and a sense of purpose. They give us something to strive for, a reason to get out of bed in the morning. When we set goals that are aligned with our values and aspirations, we tap into a deep well of motivation and inspiration.

The process of setting goals can be as simple or as complex as we choose. It might involve writing down a list of our dreams and desires, creating a vision board, or developing a detailed action plan. The key is to be specific, measurable, achievable, relevant, and time-bound (SMART). For example, instead of saying, "I want to be happy," we might say, "I want to spend at least 30 minutes each day doing something that brings me joy."

Visualization is another powerful tool for creating our future. By vividly imagining ourselves achieving our goals, we create a mental blueprint that can guide our actions and decisions. Visualization can also help to reduce anxiety and increase confidence, as we mentally rehearse the steps we need to take to reach our desired outcomes.

Creating a life that aligns with our values and aspirations is an ongoing process. It requires us to be mindful of our choices, to prioritize the things that truly matter to us, and to let go of the things that no longer serve us. It's about living a life that is authentic, meaningful, and fulfilling.

One way to align our lives with our values is to identify our core values, the guiding principles that shape our beliefs and behaviors. This might involve asking ourselves questions like:

- What is most important to me?
- What do I stand for?
- What kind of person do I want to be?

Once we have identified our core values, we can start to make choices that are in alignment with them. This might involve changing our careers, our relationships, or even our daily routines. It might also involve setting boundaries with people or situations that are not supportive of our values.

Creating a life that aligns with our values and aspirations is a journey of self-discovery. It's about learning who we are, what we want, and what truly matters to us. It's about letting go of the expectations of others and embracing our own unique path. It's about creating a life that is authentic, meaningful, and fulfilling.

Self-Reflection Questions:

1. What are the dominant narratives I tell myself about my life and who I am? Are these narratives empowering or limiting?

2. How have past traumas shaped my self-perception and beliefs about myself? Do I see myself as a victim or a survivor?

3. What strengths and resources have I developed as a result of my experiences? How can I leverage these strengths to create a more empowering narrative?

4. What kind of future do I envision for myself? What are my goals, dreams, and aspirations?

5. What steps can I take to align my life with my values and create a new chapter that reflects my true self?

Transformative Exercises:

1. **Narrative Reframing:** Identify a negative or limiting belief about yourself that stems from a past trauma. Write down this belief and then challenge it with evidence to the contrary. For example, if you believe "I am unlovable," you might counter it with evidence of people who love and care for you.

2. **Future Self Visualization:** Close your eyes and imagine yourself five years from now, having achieved your goals and living a life that is aligned with your values. What does this version of you look like? How does it feel? What are you doing? Write down your vision in detail and create a plan for how you can start working towards it today.

3. **Gratitude Journaling:** Each day, write down three things you are grateful for, focusing on the positive aspects of your life. This practice can help to shift your

perspective from negativity to appreciation, fostering a more empowering narrative.

4. **Affirmations:** Write down a list of positive affirmations that resonate with you and reflect the qualities you want to embody. Repeat these affirmations daily, either out loud or in your mind, to reprogram your subconscious mind and cultivate a more positive self-image.

5. **Vision Board:** Create a vision board that represents your ideal future. Gather images, quotes, and other inspiring materials that reflect your goals, dreams, and aspirations. Place your vision board somewhere you will see it often, allowing it to serve as a daily reminder of the future you are creating.

Chapter 10: Finding Peace in the Present Moment

"Peace is not something you wish for; it's something you make, something you do, something you are, and something you give away." – Robert Fulghum

The present moment is the only reality we truly have. The past is a memory, the future a projection, but the present is where life unfolds, where joy and pain intermingle, where healing can truly begin. For those who have known the sting of trauma, the present can often feel like a battleground, a constant struggle to outrun the ghosts of the past or quell the anxieties of the future. But within the embrace of the present moment lies a profound opportunity for peace, a sanctuary of stillness where we can finally lay down our burdens and find respite from the relentless churn of our minds.

The concept of being present is not a novel one. Ancient wisdom traditions have long extolled the virtues of mindfulness, meditation, and other practices that anchor us in the here and now. But in our fast-paced, technology-driven world, where distractions abound and the mind is constantly bombarded with stimuli, the art of being present has become increasingly elusive.

For those who have experienced trauma, the challenges of being present can be even greater. Trauma often leaves us feeling disconnected from our bodies, our emotions, and the world around us. We may find ourselves ruminating on the past or worrying about the future, our minds racing with anxious thoughts and painful memories. The present moment, with its inherent unpredictability and potential for triggering, can feel like a minefield, fraught with danger and uncertainty.

But it is precisely in the present moment, in the raw and messy reality of our experience, that healing can occur. By cultivating a gentle awareness of our thoughts, emotions, and bodily sensations, we can begin to create a space of acceptance and compassion within ourselves. We can learn to observe our pain without judgment, to acknowledge our triggers without reacting to them, and to embrace the full spectrum of our human experience.

Gratitude is a powerful tool for finding peace in the present moment. When we focus on the things we are thankful for, we shift our attention away from lack and scarcity towards abundance and appreciation. We recognize the blessings that surround us, the simple joys of life that can easily be overlooked in the midst of suffering. Gratitude can be cultivated through a daily practice of journaling, where we write down three things we are grateful for each day, or through a simple mindful pause to appreciate the beauty of nature, the warmth of the sun on our skin, or the sound of a loved one's laughter.

Another key to finding peace in the present is the art of letting go. This doesn't mean suppressing our emotions or pretending that we are not hurting. It means allowing our feelings to flow through us without clinging to them, without letting them define us. It means recognizing that our thoughts and emotions are like clouds passing through the sky, constantly changing and evolving. By learning to let go of our attachment to these transient experiences, we can find a deeper sense of peace and freedom.

Acceptance is also an essential ingredient in the recipe for peace. When we resist what is, when we fight against the reality of our experiences, we create internal conflict and suffering. But when we accept what is, with all its imperfections and challenges, we open ourselves up to the possibility of peace and serenity. This doesn't mean that we resign ourselves to a life of misery or that we give up on our dreams and aspirations. It simply means that we acknowledge the present moment as it is, without judgment or resistance.

Mindfulness practices, such as meditation, yoga, and deep breathing, can be invaluable tools for cultivating presence, gratitude, and acceptance. These practices help us to slow down, to tune into our bodies, and to observe our thoughts and emotions without getting caught up in them. They provide us with a much-needed respite from the constant chatter of the mind, allowing us to connect with the stillness and peace that reside within.

Gratitude: The Key to Contentment

"Gratitude turns what we have into enough." – Melody Beattie

In the quest for healing from the unforgettables scars of the past, we often find ourselves entangled in a web of pain, regret, and longing for what could have been. Our minds become fixated on the losses we've endured, the injustices we've faced, and the dreams that have been shattered. This focus on negativity can be all-consuming, leaving little room for joy, contentment, or peace. But what if there were a simple yet profound practice that could shift our focus from pain to appreciation, from lack to abundance, from despair to hope? That practice is gratitude.

Gratitude is not about denying the reality of our pain or pretending that everything is perfect. It's about recognizing the good that exists in our lives, even amidst the challenges and setbacks. It's about acknowledging the blessings we often take for granted, the small moments of joy that can easily be overlooked in the midst of suffering.

Scientific research supports the transformative power of gratitude. Studies have shown that practicing gratitude can reduce stress, anxiety, and depression, while increasing happiness, resilience, and overall well-being. It can also improve sleep, boost the immune system, and enhance our relationships with others. For those who have experienced trauma, gratitude can be a particularly powerful tool for healing, as it helps to shift our focus from the pain of the past to the possibilities of the present.

The practice of gratitude is not about Pollyannaish optimism or denying the difficult realities of life. It's about choosing to focus on the good, even when things are tough. It's about recognizing that even in the darkest of times, there is always something to be grateful for. This might be the warmth of the sun on our skin, the sound of birdsong, the love of a friend or family member, or simply the fact that we are alive and breathing.

Gratitude can be cultivated through a variety of practices. One simple yet effective practice is to keep a gratitude journal. Each day, take a few moments to write down three things you are grateful for. These can be big or small, concrete or abstract. The key is to focus on the positive aspects of your life, however fleeting or seemingly insignificant they may be.

Another powerful gratitude practice is to write a letter of gratitude to someone who has made a positive impact on your life. Express your appreciation for their kindness, support, or guidance. This can be a transformative experience, not just for the recipient of the letter, but also for yourself, as you reflect on the positive influences in your life.

You can also practice gratitude through simple acts of kindness towards others. Expressing appreciation to a stranger, offering a helping hand to someone in need, or simply smiling at someone can all create a ripple effect of positivity and connection. By focusing on giving to others, we shift our attention away from our own problems and cultivate a sense of gratitude for the opportunity to make a difference in the world.

The practice of gratitude is not always easy, especially when we are in the midst of pain or suffering. But even in the darkest of times, there is always something to be grateful for. It might be the support of a loved one, the strength we find within ourselves, or simply the opportunity to learn and grow from our experiences.

By cultivating gratitude, we can begin to rewire our brains, training them to focus on the positive rather than the negative. We can shift our attention away from the pain of the past and towards the possibilities of the present. We can discover that even in the face of adversity, there is always something to be thankful for, and that gratitude is the key to unlocking a deeper sense of contentment, joy, and inner peace.

The Art of Letting Go: Surrendering to What Is

> *"Some things cannot be fixed. They can only be carried." - Megan Devine*

The weight of the past can feel like a millstone around our necks, dragging us down into the depths of despair. We cling to our pain, our regrets, our anger, as if they were life rafts in a turbulent sea. But what if, in our desperate grasp, we are actually preventing ourselves from finding solid ground? What if, by learning to let go, to surrender to the flow of life, we could discover a newfound sense of peace and freedom?

Acceptance and surrender, often misunderstood as passive resignation, are in fact powerful tools for healing and transformation. They are not about giving up or denying the reality of our pain, but rather about acknowledging what is, without judgment or resistance. It's about recognizing that we cannot change the past, but we can choose how we respond to it in the present moment.

The concept of acceptance is deeply rooted in various spiritual and philosophical traditions. In Buddhism, acceptance is a central tenet of the Eightfold Path, the path to enlightenment. It involves acknowledging the impermanence of all things, the inevitability of suffering, and the interconnectedness of all beings. By accepting these truths, we can free ourselves from the illusion of control and find peace in the midst of chaos.

Surrender, on the other hand, is often associated with weakness or defeat. But in the context of healing, surrender is not about giving up; it's about letting go of the struggle, the resistance, the need to control. It's about trusting that life has a wisdom beyond our own understanding, a plan that is unfolding even in the midst of our pain.

Releasing attachment to the past is a crucial step in the process of acceptance and surrender. When we cling to our pain, our regrets, our anger, we keep ourselves tethered to the past, preventing us from fully embracing the present moment. This attachment can manifest in various ways, from ruminating on past events to harboring resentment towards those who have hurt us.

But by learning to let go, to release the stories we tell ourselves about the past, we can free ourselves from the chains of our own making. We can open ourselves up to the possibility of forgiveness, both of ourselves and others. We can begin to see our experiences in a new light, as opportunities for growth and learning, rather than sources of shame or regret.

Embracing the present moment is another key aspect of acceptance and surrender. When we are fully present, we are not dwelling on the past or worrying about the future. We are simply here, now, experiencing life as it unfolds. This present-moment awareness allows us to connect with the richness and fullness of our experience, to appreciate the simple joys of life, and to find peace amidst the chaos.

Mindfulness practices, such as meditation, yoga, and deep breathing, can be invaluable tools for cultivating presence, acceptance, and surrender. These practices help us to slow down, to tune into our bodies, and to observe our thoughts and emotions without judgment. They teach us to be kind and compassionate towards ourselves, to acknowledge our pain without letting it consume us.

Releasing attachment to the past and embracing the present moment is not an overnight process. It takes time, patience, and practice. There will be moments when the old patterns resurface, when the pain feels overwhelming, and when the urge to cling to the past is strong. But with each act of surrender, with each conscious choice to embrace the present moment, we move closer to a place of inner peace and freedom.

We begin to see that the past, while it may have shaped us, does not define us. We recognize that we are not our wounds, but rather the sum of our experiences, both light and dark. We discover that within every challenge, within every setback, lies an opportunity for growth and transformation.

In the words of the poet Rumi, "The wound is the place where the Light enters you." By embracing our pain, by surrendering to the flow of life, we allow the light of healing to enter our hearts, illuminating the path to wholeness and peace.

Self-Reflection Questions:

1. When do I feel most at peace? What activities, environments, or people help me to feel

grounded and centered in the present moment?

2. What are some of the biggest obstacles to my inner peace? Are there specific thoughts, emotions, or situations that trigger anxiety, worry, or rumination?

3. How often do I express gratitude in my daily life? Do I actively seek out things to be thankful for, or do I tend to focus on what's lacking?

4. What does surrender mean to me? Am I willing to let go of the need for control and trust in the unfolding of life?

5. How can I cultivate a deeper sense of acceptance towards myself, my experiences, and the world around me?

Transformative Exercises:

1. **Gratitude Jar:** Find a jar or container and decorate it as you wish. Each day, write down one thing you are grateful for on a small piece

of paper and place it in the jar. At the end of the week or month, read through the notes and reflect on all the blessings in your life.

2. **Mindful Breathing Meditation:** Find a comfortable seated position and close your eyes. Bring your attention to your breath, noticing the sensation of the air entering and leaving your nostrils or the rise and fall of your abdomen. If your mind wanders, gently guide it back to your breath. Continue for 5-10 minutes, allowing yourself to simply be present with your breath.

3. **Nature Immersion:** Spend time in nature, whether it's a walk in the park, a hike in the woods, or simply sitting under a tree. Engage your senses fully, noticing the sights, sounds, smells, and textures around you. Allow yourself to be fully present in the natural world, letting go of any worries or distractions.

4. **Acceptance Meditation:** Find a quiet space and sit comfortably. Close your eyes and bring to mind a situation or experience that you are struggling to accept. Acknowledge the feelings that arise, allowing yourself to feel them fully without judgment. Then, repeat to yourself, "I accept this moment as it is. I am open to what is happening right now." Continue to repeat this phrase, allowing yourself to surrender to the present moment.

5. **Acts of Kindness:** Practice small acts of kindness towards others, such as holding a door open for someone, offering a compliment, or volunteering your time. By focusing on giving to others, you can shift your attention away from your own problems and cultivate a sense of gratitude and connection.

Chapter 11: Building a Life of Peace and Purpose

"The purpose of our lives is to be happy." – Dalai Lama

As we heal from the unforgettables of the past, we begin to carve a new path, one that is not dictated by our wounds, but rather illuminated by our newfound wisdom and resilience. This path leads us towards a life of peace and purpose, a life where we are not merely surviving, but thriving. It's a life where our past experiences, though never forgotten, no longer hold us hostage, but instead serve as stepping stones towards a more fulfilling and joyful existence.

Building a life of peace and purpose is not a destination, but an ongoing journey. It's a continuous process of self-discovery, growth, and alignment with our core values. It's about creating a life that is authentic, meaningful, and deeply satisfying. It's about living in harmony with ourselves, with others, and with the world around us.

Living in alignment with our values is a cornerstone of a peaceful and purposeful life. When our actions reflect our deepest beliefs and principles, we experience a sense of integrity and congruency. We feel a deep satisfaction knowing that we are living in accordance with our true selves. But how do we identify our values? It often starts with introspection, with asking ourselves questions like:

- What matters most to me?

- What do I stand for?

- What kind of impact do I want to have on the world?

The answers to these questions can reveal our core values, the guiding principles that shape our choices and actions. Once we have identified our values, we can begin to make conscious decisions that align with them. This might involve changing our careers, our relationships, or even our daily routines. It might also mean setting boundaries, saying no to things that don't serve us, and prioritizing the things that truly matter.

Living in alignment with our values is not always easy. It can require us to make difficult choices, to step outside of our comfort zones, and to challenge the expectations of others. But the rewards are immeasurable. When we live in alignment with our values, we experience a deep sense of fulfillment, purpose, and inner peace.

Finding our purpose is another essential aspect of building a life of peace. Purpose is that deep-seated sense of meaning and direction that gives our lives significance. It's the reason we get out of bed in the morning, the driving force behind our actions and decisions. When we have a sense of purpose, we feel more connected to ourselves, to others, and to the world around us. We experience a greater sense of satisfaction, fulfillment, and well-being.

Discovering our purpose is a journey of exploration and experimentation. It often involves trying new things, stepping outside of our comfort zones, and listening to our intuition. It might mean reflecting on our passions, our talents, and the things that bring us joy. It might also involve considering the needs of others and how we can contribute to the greater good.

Purpose can be found in a variety of places. It might be in our careers, our relationships, our hobbies, our creative pursuits, or our volunteer work. It might be in our spiritual practices, our connection to nature, or our commitment to social justice. The key is to find something that resonates with us, something that ignites our passion and fuels our desire to make a difference in the world.

When we live a life of peace and purpose, we become a beacon of light for others. We inspire those around us to live more authentically, to pursue their dreams, and to make a positive impact on the world. We create a ripple effect of positivity and transformation, contributing to the healing of not just ourselves, but also our communities and the world at large.

Building a life of peace and purpose is not a solo endeavor. It's a journey that is best undertaken with the support and guidance of others. This might involve seeking out mentors, coaches, or therapists who can help us to identify our values, discover our purpose, and navigate the challenges that inevitably arise along the way. It might also involve connecting with a community of like-minded individuals who share our values and aspirations.

The journey to healing what we can't forget is a transformative one. It's a journey that takes us from the depths of despair to the heights of hope and possibility. By living in alignment with our values, finding our purpose, and cultivating a sense of inner peace, we can create a life that is not defined by our past traumas, but rather by our resilience, our strength, and our capacity for love and joy.

Living in Alignment with Your Values

"When your values are clear to you, making decisions becomes easier." – Roy E. Disney

In the journey to heal what we can't forget, a profound shift occurs – a shift from being defined by our past traumas to being guided by our innermost values. This transformative process involves more than just letting go of the past; it's about consciously crafting a life that reflects who we truly are, a life that resonates with our deepest beliefs and aspirations.

Living in alignment with our values is a cornerstone of lasting well-being. It's about creating a life that feels authentic, meaningful, and deeply satisfying. When our actions reflect our core values, we experience a sense of integrity and congruency, a feeling that we are living in accordance with our true selves. This alignment fosters a sense of inner peace, a sense of purpose, and a deep-seated contentment that cannot be found in external validation or material possessions.

But what exactly are values? Values are our guiding principles, the compass that directs our choices and actions. They are the things that matter most to us, the qualities we strive to embody, and the ideals we hold dear. Values can be personal, cultural, or spiritual, and they can vary greatly from person to person. Some common values include honesty, integrity, compassion, creativity, adventure, family, and community.

Identifying our core values is a crucial step in creating a life that reflects who we truly are. It's a process of self-discovery, of uncovering the beliefs and principles that resonate most deeply with us. One way to begin this process is to reflect on the moments in our lives when we felt most alive, most fulfilled, most aligned with our true selves. What were we doing? Who were we with? What values were we embodying in those moments?

Another approach is to consider the people we admire, those who inspire us with their actions and character. What qualities do they possess that we value? What principles do they live by that resonate with us? By reflecting on our own experiences and the examples of others, we can begin to identify the values that are most important to us.

Once we have identified our core values, we can begin to examine how well our lives reflect those values. Are our actions consistent with our beliefs? Are we spending our time and energy on things that truly matter to us? Are we living a life that is authentic and meaningful?

If the answer to any of these questions is no, then it may be time to make some changes. This doesn't necessarily mean making drastic changes overnight. It can start with small steps, such as incorporating more of our values into our daily routines, setting boundaries with people or situations that don't align with our values, or making choices that reflect our priorities.

Living in alignment with our values is an ongoing process. It requires constant self-reflection, a willingness to challenge our assumptions, and a commitment to making choices that honor our deepest beliefs and aspirations. But the rewards are worth it. When we live in alignment with our values, we experience a greater sense of purpose, fulfillment, and inner peace. We also tend to have stronger relationships, better health, and a more positive outlook on life.

Moreover, living in alignment with our values can be a powerful antidote to the lingering effects of trauma. Trauma can often leave us feeling disconnected from ourselves, our values, and our purpose in life. But by consciously choosing to live a life that reflects our values, we can reclaim our power, rebuild our sense of self, and create a more meaningful and fulfilling future.

Imagine a life where your actions are guided by your deepest beliefs, where your choices reflect your priorities, and where your days are filled with activities that bring you joy and fulfillment. This is the life that is possible when you live in alignment with your values. It's a life of authenticity, purpose, and deep-seated contentment. It's a life that is worth striving for.

Service to Others: Healing Through Helping

"Our prime purpose in this life is to help others. And if you can't help them, at least don't hurt them." – Dalai Lama

In the intricate dance of healing, a profound truth emerges: the act of helping others can be a potent balm for our own wounds. This reciprocal exchange, where compassion flows both outward and inward, is a testament to the interconnectedness of the human experience. When we extend a helping hand to those in need, we not only uplift their spirits, but we also nourish our own souls, fostering a sense of purpose, connection, and belonging that can be transformative in the face of adversity.

Research supports the notion that helping others can be a powerful catalyst for healing. Studies have shown that volunteering, acts of kindness, and other forms of service can reduce stress, boost mood, and enhance overall well-being. For individuals who have experienced trauma, helping others can be particularly beneficial, as it can help to shift focus away from personal pain and towards a sense of purpose and connection to something larger than oneself.

The act of helping others can take many forms. It can be as simple as offering a listening ear to a friend in need, volunteering at a local shelter, or donating to a cause you believe in. It can also involve using your unique talents and skills to make a difference in the world, whether it's through teaching, mentoring, advocating for change, or simply spreading kindness and compassion wherever you go.

The key is to find a way to give back that resonates with your values and interests. Perhaps you have a passion for animal welfare, environmental conservation, or social justice. Maybe you have a talent for music, art, or writing that you can use to uplift and inspire others. Or perhaps you simply enjoy connecting with people and offering a listening ear or a helping hand.

By finding ways to serve others, we tap into a deep well of compassion and empathy within ourselves. We begin to see the world through a different lens, one that is less focused on our own problems and more attuned to the needs of others. This shift in perspective can be incredibly healing, as it allows us to move beyond our own pain and connect with a greater sense of purpose and meaning.

The act of helping others can also foster a sense of connection and belonging. When we work alongside others towards a common goal, we create bonds of friendship and solidarity. We feel a sense of shared purpose, a reminder that we are not alone in our struggles. This sense of connection can be incredibly empowering, providing us with the support and encouragement we need to overcome adversity and thrive.

Moreover, helping others can be a powerful antidote to the feelings of helplessness and powerlessness that often accompany trauma. When we take action to make a positive difference in the world, we reclaim our agency and our ability to effect change. We discover that we have the power to make a difference, no matter how small, and that our contributions matter.

Of course, it's important to be mindful of our own needs and limitations. Helping others should not come at the expense of our own well-being. It's important to set boundaries, to say no when we need to, and to prioritize our own self-care. When we are well-rested, nourished, and emotionally balanced, we are better able to show up for others in a meaningful and sustainable way.

Finding purpose in service is not about becoming a martyr or sacrificing our own needs for the sake of others. It's about finding a way to give back that is both fulfilling and sustainable. It's about recognizing that our own well-being is inextricably linked to the well-being of others, and that by helping others, we are also helping ourselves.

As you embark on your own healing journey, consider how you can incorporate service to others into your life. Look for opportunities to volunteer your time, talents, or resources. Reach out to those in need, offer a listening ear, or simply spread kindness and compassion wherever you go. Remember, the act of helping others is not just a selfless act; it's a powerful tool for healing and transformation, a way to reconnect with our humanity, to find meaning and purpose, and to create a more compassionate and just world.

Chapter 12: The Ongoing Journey: Maintaining Your Peace

The path to healing from trauma is not a sprint, but a marathon. It's a winding road with twists and turns, uphill climbs and gentle descents. There will be moments of triumph, where we feel empowered and free, and moments of setback, where the weight of the past threatens to drag us down. But with each step we take, with each challenge we overcome, we move closer to a life of sustained peace and well-being.

Maintaining this newfound peace is an ongoing journey, a lifelong commitment to ourselves and our healing. It's about nurturing the seeds of resilience we've planted, tending to the garden of our well-being, and staying vigilant against the weeds of old patterns and triggers that may try to resurface.

Just as a gardener must remain vigilant against pests and weeds that threaten to overrun their carefully cultivated plants, so too must we be mindful of the triggers that can disrupt our hard-won peace. These triggers can be external, such as reminders of past trauma or stressful situations, or internal, such as negative self-talk or self-doubt.

Learning to identify our triggers is a crucial step in maintaining our peace. By recognizing the situations, people, or thoughts that tend to activate our stress response, we can develop strategies for managing them. This might involve setting boundaries, practicing mindfulness techniques, or seeking support from loved ones or professionals.

Setbacks are an inevitable part of the healing journey. There will be days when the pain feels overwhelming, when the old wounds threaten to reopen, and when we question our progress. It's important to remember that these setbacks are not failures, but rather opportunities for growth and learning. They are reminders that healing is not a linear process, but a cyclical one, with periods of progress and regression.

By reframing setbacks as opportunities for growth, we can learn to embrace them as part of the journey. We can use them to deepen our self-awareness, to identify areas where we need additional support, and to strengthen our resilience muscles.

The practice of self-compassion is essential for navigating setbacks. When we stumble or fall, it's important to treat ourselves with kindness and understanding, rather than self-criticism or judgment. We need to remind ourselves that we are human, imperfect, and that mistakes are an inevitable part of the learning process.

Maintaining our peace also requires us to prioritize self-care. Just as a car needs regular maintenance to run smoothly, so too do our minds, bodies, and spirits need regular nourishment and care to function optimally. This might involve establishing a daily routine that includes mindfulness practices, exercise, healthy eating, and adequate sleep. It might also involve setting aside time for activities that bring us joy and relaxation, such as spending time in nature, pursuing creative hobbies, or connecting with loved ones.

In the words of the Buddha, "You yourself, as much as anybody in the entire universe, deserve your love and affection." By prioritizing our own well-being, we are not being selfish; we are simply honoring our own worth and recognizing that we are worthy of love, care, and compassion.

The journey to maintaining our peace is not a solitary one. It's a journey best undertaken with the support and guidance of others. This might involve seeking out therapy, joining a support group, or simply connecting with loved ones who can offer empathy, encouragement, and a listening ear.

By surrounding ourselves with a supportive network, we create a safety net that can catch us when we fall, a community that can uplift us when we are down, and a source of inspiration that can motivate us to keep moving forward.

Relapse Prevention: Navigating Triggers and Challenges

> *"The wound is healed, but the scar remains." - Benjamin Disraeli*

The journey of healing from trauma is not a linear path, nor is it a destination that can be reached and forgotten. It's an ongoing process, a lifelong commitment to self-care, awareness, and vigilance. Even after significant progress has been made, the echoes of the past can resurface, triggered by seemingly innocuous events or subtle shifts in our internal landscape. These triggers, while often unwelcome, are not a sign of failure or regression. They are simply reminders of the wounds we carry, a call to revisit the tools and strategies that have helped us heal thus far.

Triggers can take many forms, varying from person to person and depending on the nature of the trauma experienced. They can be external, such as specific sights, sounds, smells, or situations that remind us of the traumatic event. For example, a war veteran might be triggered by the sound of fireworks, a survivor of sexual assault might be triggered by a certain type of cologne, or a person who experienced a car accident might be triggered by the sight of a similar vehicle.

Triggers can also be internal, arising from thoughts, emotions, or bodily sensations. For instance, feelings of anxiety, anger, or sadness can trigger memories of past trauma. Similarly, physical sensations like a racing heart, shortness of breath, or muscle tension can also be cues that our bodies are responding to a perceived threat.

Recognizing and understanding our triggers is a crucial step in relapse prevention. By identifying the situations, people, or thoughts that tend to activate our stress response, we can develop strategies for managing them. This might involve avoiding certain triggers altogether, if possible, or learning to tolerate them through gradual exposure and desensitization techniques.

One effective strategy for managing triggers is to create a "safety plan." This plan outlines specific steps you can take when you feel triggered, such as reaching out to a trusted friend or therapist, practicing relaxation techniques, or engaging in activities that bring you joy and comfort. Having a plan in place can help you to feel more prepared and empowered when faced with a trigger, reducing the likelihood of relapse.

Another important aspect of relapse prevention is ongoing self-care. Just as a garden needs regular tending to thrive, so too does our emotional well-being require ongoing nourishment and attention. This might involve prioritizing healthy habits such as getting enough sleep, eating nutritious foods, exercising regularly, and engaging in activities that bring us joy and relaxation.

Self-care also involves cultivating a strong support network of friends, family members, or professionals who can offer us encouragement, guidance, and a listening ear. It's important to remember that we don't have to go through this journey alone. Reaching out for help is a sign of strength, not weakness.

Mindfulness practices, such as meditation, yoga, and deep breathing, can also be invaluable tools for relapse prevention. By cultivating present-moment awareness, we can learn to observe our thoughts and emotions without judgment, reducing their power to trigger us. Mindfulness can also help us to develop a greater sense of self-compassion, allowing us to be kind and understanding towards ourselves when we do experience setbacks.

It's important to remember that healing is not a linear process. There will be ups and downs, good days and bad days. There may be times when we feel like we are taking two steps forward and one step back. But with each challenge we overcome, with each trigger we manage, we strengthen our resilience and move closer to a life of sustained peace and well-being.

The Gift of Healing: Sharing Your Wisdom

"A candle loses nothing by lighting another candle." - James Keller

In the tapestry of human experience, stories are the threads that connect us, the bridges that span the chasms of isolation and pain. When we share our stories of healing, we not only illuminate our own path, but we also light the way for others who are stumbling in the darkness. The gift of healing is not meant to be hoarded; it's meant to be shared, to be passed on like a torch from one weary traveler to another.

Research has shown that sharing our stories can have a profound impact on our well-being. It can reduce feelings of shame and isolation, increase self-esteem, and foster a sense of connection and belonging. For those who have experienced trauma, sharing our stories can be especially transformative. It can help us to make sense of our experiences, to integrate them into our lives, and to move forward with a renewed sense of purpose and meaning.

But the benefits of sharing our stories extend far beyond our own personal healing. When we share our experiences, we offer a beacon of hope to others who are struggling. We show them that they are not alone, that healing is possible, and that there is light at the end of the tunnel. We inspire them to take the first step on their own healing journey, to reach out for help, and to believe in their own capacity for resilience and recovery.

The ripple effect of sharing our stories can be truly remarkable. One person's story can inspire another, and that person's story can inspire yet another, creating a chain reaction of healing and transformation. By sharing our wisdom, we become catalysts for change, not just in our own lives, but in the lives of countless others.

There are many ways to share our stories and wisdom. We can write about our experiences in a journal, blog, or even a book. We can share our stories in support groups, online forums, or other communities where others are also on the path to healing. We can speak out about our experiences at conferences, workshops, or other public events. We can even mentor others who are just starting their healing journey, offering guidance, support, and encouragement.

The key is to find a way to share your story that feels authentic and empowering to you. There is no right or wrong way to do it. Some people prefer to write anonymously, while others feel comfortable sharing their stories publicly. Some people prefer to share their experiences in a group setting, while others prefer one-on-one conversations.

The most important thing is to find a way to share your story that feels safe and supportive. This might involve seeking out communities or individuals who you trust and who understand your experiences. It might also involve setting boundaries around what you are willing to share and how you want to share it.

Remember, sharing your story is not about seeking pity or attention. It's about offering hope and inspiration to others, about creating a ripple effect of healing and transformation. It's about using your voice to make a difference in the world.

Sharing your wisdom can take many forms. It might involve offering advice and guidance based on your own experiences, sharing resources and information you have found helpful, or simply listening with empathy and compassion to others who are struggling. It's about using your knowledge and experience to help others on their own healing journeys.

The act of sharing our wisdom can be deeply rewarding. It allows us to connect with others on a deeper level, to foster a sense of community and belonging, and to make a positive impact on the world. It can also deepen our own healing, as we reflect on our experiences and gain new insights into our own journey.

As you continue on your path to healing, consider how you can share your story and wisdom with others. Whether it's through writing, speaking, mentoring, or simply offering a listening ear, your voice has the power to inspire and empower others. By sharing your journey, you can create a ripple effect of healing that extends far beyond yourself, touching countless lives and making the world a brighter place.

Remember, the gift of healing is not meant to be kept to yourself. It's meant to be shared, to be passed on, to be a source of light and hope for others who are also on the path to recovery.

Conclusion: Embrace Your Healing Journey

"The wound is not my fault, but the healing is my responsibility." - Rune Lazuli

As we approach the end of this journey together, we stand on the precipice of a new beginning. The pages of this book have guided us through the complex landscape of healing, offering tools, insights, and strategies to transform our relationship with the past and create a more peaceful and fulfilling present.

We have explored the many faces of trauma, from the dramatic and life-altering events that shatter our sense of safety, to the subtle, insidious wounds that erode our self-worth. We have learned that trauma, regardless of its form or intensity, leaves an imprint on our minds, bodies, and spirits, shaping our thoughts, emotions, and behaviors.

We have discovered that healing is not about erasing the past or pretending that the pain didn't happen. It's about acknowledging our wounds, honoring our experiences, and finding ways to integrate them into our lives. It's about releasing the grip of the past, embracing our pain as a teacher, and cultivating self-compassion.

We have learned that healing is a journey, not a destination. It's an ongoing process of self-discovery, growth, and transformation. It requires patience, perseverance, and a willingness to face our deepest fears and vulnerabilities. But the rewards are immeasurable.

Through the practice of mindfulness, we have learned to anchor ourselves in the present moment, to observe our thoughts and emotions without judgment, and to find a sense of peace amidst the chaos. We have discovered the power of self-compassion, the antidote to self-blame and shame. We have learned to nurture our bodies and minds, to create a safe and supportive environment where healing can flourish.

We have also explored the transformative power of connection, the importance of building a support network of trusted friends, family members, or professionals who can offer us guidance, encouragement, and a listening ear. We have discovered the strength and resilience that can be found in community, the healing that can occur when we share our stories and connect with others who understand our experiences.

We have learned that the journey of healing is not just about recovering from the past; it's also about creating a brighter future. By reframing our narratives, envisioning a future free from the constraints of our past traumas, and living in alignment with our values, we can build a life that is authentic, meaningful, and deeply satisfying.

As you continue on your healing journey, remember that you are not alone. There are countless others who have walked this path before you, who have faced similar challenges and emerged stronger and wiser. Reach out to them, share your stories, and offer your support. Remember, the gift of healing is not meant to be hoarded; it's meant to be shared.

Celebrate your progress, no matter how small. Each step you take towards healing is a victory, a testament to your courage and resilience. Be kind to yourself, patient with yourself, and trust in the process. Healing is not always easy, but it is always possible.

And as you move forward, remember the words of the poet Rumi: "The wound is the place where the Light enters you." Your wounds, though painful, can also be a source of strength, wisdom, and compassion. Embrace them, learn from them, and allow them to illuminate your path to a brighter future.

PLEASE LEAVE AN HONEST REVIEW

If the journey within these pages has resonated with you, stirred your soul, or sparked a flicker of hope, I invite you to share your experience. Your honest review on platforms like Amazon can illuminate the path for others seeking healing. Every word you share is a beacon of light, a testament to the power of resilience and the unwavering spirit of the human heart. Your review is more than just feedback; it's a gift to fellow travelers on the road to recovery.